Keep it
in the family

Keep it in the family

Resources for all age worship
Stuart Thomas

Kevin
Mayhew

First published in 1993 by
KEVIN MAYHEW LTD
Rattlesden
Bury St Edmunds
Suffolk IP30 0SZ

ISBN 0 86209 444 5

Front Cover: *The Sunday Lesson* by Thomas Herbert Maguire (1821–1895).
Reproduced by courtesy of Haynes Fine Art,
Broadway/Fine Art Photographic Library, London.

Cover design by Juliette Clarke and Graham Johnstone
Typesetting and Page Creation by Anglia Photoset Ltd
Printed and bound in Great Britain.

Contents

Foreword

I like to think I'm not too old, but I can still remember the days when children weren't welcome in 'grown-up' services. We were hived off to a special 'children's church', which was in the same 'hymn sandwich' format, but with a children's address by a guest speaker. Occasionally these were memorable and entertaining, but mostly as dull as ditchwater. Rarely can I remember either the worship or the ministry of the word being exciting or spiritually uplifting, and I grew up under the naive impression that this was the norm. Only in my early twenties did I realise that worship isn't something we do to or for God, because he'll get cross if we don't. Instead I began to experience worship as entering into the worship of Heaven, being caught up in the praise of all creation, as the greatest thing I can ever do.

Today, children and young people are leaving the Church at a rate of knots. There's nothing to hold them. The values preached are no longer accepted by much of society, and its attitudes and practises seem to them to be part of a dying culture that they've rejected. Unless the Church addresses this issue soon, it will become even more marginalised as a tiny sect, fascinating culturally but of no use to anyone, except as a social agency.

This book is hardly going to solve the Church's problems overnight, but it does point to a way forward which many have already started to follow. All-age worship enables the whole church family to come together for an act of worship. Those who are two or ninety-two years old can be drawn into God's presence and experience more of his love and grace. Flexibility is the keynote, because it enables variety to be built in. After all, why would God want our worship to be boring? He gave us our creative urge and the facility to respond to beauty and colour and sound. Dreary services are quite unworthy of our great and infinite God, who gave the universe such rich variety.

The specimen services in these pages aren't meant to be rigidly adhered to, but to be used to enrich and enliven all-age worship. Most of them have been 'road-tested' but can be adapted for different contexts and places. The tradition within which you live and worship may well dictate some alterations to accommodate local needs.

In a day when families are splintering apart and dislocated, the Church needs to do all it can to help families and single people to worship together. Each generation has so much to gain from others that it is a waste not to harness that resource for everyone's benefit. If this book enables a step to be taken along the road towards making that happen effectively then it will have met its purpose.

Families and Services

It's the first Tuesday of the month – PCC night at St Grump's. The highlight of the evening's agenda is a discussion on 'Family Services', instigated by the vicar (who's had his ear bent by two young families who don't find 1662 Mattins a great attraction for small children). St Grump's is an old church, formerly the centre of a village community. Things have changed, however, and a large new housing estate has been built, trebling the size of the parish. Most of its residents are young couples and families, whose allegiance is more with the neighbouring town. Unfortunately, few if any of these are churchgoers. Those who do so probably drive to one of the town churches. Christmas services see a slight increase in attendance, and the building is full when the local church school has a special service. Otherwise, the regular congregation is becoming older and, as its stalwarts ail or die, numbers are declining.

Let it be said in fairness that everyone on the PCC is concerned about this situation and wants to see more young people worshipping at St Grump's. How to achieve this is another issue. Miss Baulk, a member for twenty-seven years (and likely to remain so for another twenty-seven!) deplores the deteriorating standards of behaviour in the young these days. Colonel Bawle is concerned to preserve the rich ecclesiastical traditions in which he was brought up (and thinks everyone else should be). Mrs Trill, representing the choir, is worried that musical standards will decline. Mr Cash, the Treasurer, doesn't want to see some new project eating up financial resources which are already stretched. Mr Upfront, whose children are still living at home, thinks that St Grump's image in the wider community is poor, not least among younger folk (but then he would – he works in marketing).

Various points of view are expressed and after substantial debate the vicar is authorised to proceed on a three-month experimental basis with Family Services – provided there are no guitars, modern versions of the Lord's Prayer or hymns written after 1899. You won't be surprised to learn that the experiment hardly left the ground.

Meanwhile, on the other side of town St Hilarius the Great have also been trying out Family Services. They've not only taken off, but apparently gone into orbit! There's an eight-piece band with full sound system, and the organ is used about three times a year. Service books were abandoned two years ago, to assist 'spontaneity' in worship. The services take two hours or more and everyone goes home hoarse after singing each song six times. The vicar is occasionally seen swinging from the rafters, but not often standing in the pulpit. This task is usually assigned to a member of the congregation on the 'preaching team'. All of this team are active, committed Christians and acquit themselves with sincerity and fortitude (though not always with sensitivity or aptitude). Numbers have gone up slightly. Regrettably most of the parish has been left far behind, wondering what's happened.

The St Grump's congregation are not unlike the proverbial tortoise, far outpaced by the social and cultural changes around them. Their friends at St Hilarius the Great are more like Mr Toad with his new car, racing off into the distance before anyone's had time to blink. Yes, I'm exaggerating for effect – but only just! All over the country similar stories could be told, even if the situations are less caricatured. Both St Grump's and St Hilarius the Great have a genuine concern to make the church more accessible to young families and children, many of whom have little contact with or experience of the Christian faith. Their lack of success was not due to a lack of sincerity or faith. What they both failed to do was address the needs of the whole parish, with the result that tradition and innovation, formality and spontaneity, weren't integrated but became mutually exclusive. St Grump's weren't prepared to lose anything they already had (all change involves some loss), while St Hilarius the Great threw out the baby with the bathwater, leaving people with no familiar anchor points to hold on to.

'Family Service' is a term with surprisingly emotive overtones. For some it spells change and creates insecurity, while at the other extreme it becomes an excuse for 'going freestyle', a euphemism for 'anything goes'. However, it's quite possible to create a 'Family Service' which is both liturgically acceptable and appealing to newcomers who may be totally unfamiliar with what happens in church.

Part of the problem lies in that word 'family'. The Church has always promoted the virtues of the family, but even the most devout Christian feels ambiguous at times about his own kith and kin. A former Bishop of Peterborough was once quoted as saying that

friends "are God's way of apologising to you for your family"! Few would disagree that families should be havens of peace, security and joy, but all have experienced them at times as a churning sea of tension and anger. Some have been scarred deeply, and they cringe at the thought of worship directed at the family.

The Industrial Revolution and subsequent social developments have radically altered our attitudes to the family. Today the word makes us think first of Mum, Dad and 1.8 kids; the classic Cornflakes-for-breakfast, Freshmint toothpaste unit, who feed their dog with the most nutritious tinned food available and appear in adverts on a sunny beach taking their holidays with a non-stop smile. The nuclear family is a very recent invention, however. The Biblical concept is far more extended, including not only Grannies, Uncles and Cousins, but also slaves and servants. Paul's letter to Philemon requests him to receive Onesimus back as part of the 'household'. In fact, the term 'family of God' is used only once to describe the Church; 'household of God' is more frequently met. Even until fairly recently it was unusual for families to be widely separated. More often families would live nearby in the same community, able to help each other out with such duties as babysitting and caring for the elderly. Today grownup children are frequently miles apart from their parents, who then can't help with caring for grandchildren when the time comes. When the grandparents become infirm, their children have to put them in a home for the elderly, as they can't provide the necessary care. Parents and young children have a proper need for privacy, as do married couples; however, we should not regard the present situation as the Biblical norm.

Nor should we forget the singles in our churches, many of whom are in the older age-bracket. There are divorcees, and children of broken marriages; those who can't have children; those who've been bereaved: all of these may find it hard to worship in an environment geared exclusively to families with small children. Some of them, especially the older generation, may look on their church as a refuge of peace and security, which is under threat from rapid change.

In many ways the church mirrors the human family in its network of relationships and complex web of interactions. Significantly Paul and other New Testament writers often speak of relationships between Christians in 'family' terms – brothers and sisters, parents and children and so on. Jesus told Nicodemus that he must 'be born again' (a sadly abused term), a reminder that just as a child is born into a human family so a new Christian is born into the family of the Church. As a child grows up it does so in a family context, learning to relate to its environment and fellow humans. It's exactly the same as we grow in the Christian faith, learning to interpret that faith in terms of our world and to belong to the fellowship of believers. In a family there should be mutual love and care, support and encouragement in crises, and shared joy in happy times. Like any human family, the Church family will have its squabbles and difficulties, too. That's how we mature and grow. If a family activity is to be a success it must allow for the views and aspirations of all its members, young and old, male and

female, single and married. A true 'family service' is therefore one which caters for the spiritual needs of all the members of the congregation, not just an isolated group. 'All-age worship' is a much better description of what we should be aiming for.

What kind of service?
In an Anglican context the basic choice here is between a Eucharistic or non-Eucharistic service. In other traditions this may have less significance. Some would argue that the sacraments are for everyone, and should always be an integral part of family worship, so that children grow up familiar with them and ready to accept them. Others would respond that many of those unfamiliar with Church might be put off by a ritual they feel excluded from. Both views are valid, though personally I tend to the former view. So, incidentally do the children in our church, who reckon kneeling at the altar-rail is the best bit of the service! However, from a practical viewpoint this takes longer and changes the whole shape of the liturgy.

What shape should the service take?
By far the most important factor is that each service, whatever it contains and however regularly it takes place, should have a distinct and recognisable pattern. The Anglican Morning Prayer Service, uninspired though it may seem to some, has a clear and useful shape. An opening hymn is followed by a brief introduction and the Confession and Absolution. Then comes a Psalm, readings from Scripture and the Canticles. The Creed and Intercessions follow, with a sermon to explain the Scripture. Many alternative confessions are available today,

and innumerable collects and responsive prayers. Anglican chanting of Psalms and Canticles has largely disappeared from the parish church (except perhaps where there is a good choir), but there are many modern songs based on the Psalms and other parts of Scripture which the younger generation will sing more readily. Many parts of the ASB have in fact been set to excellent modern tunes, adding to the variety now possible in all-age worship. Far from being a straitjacket, a liturgy which has a clear structure enables the minister to use a much greater variety of material. If there are some in the congregation who aren't familiar with the ways of the Church, they will most probably find it easier to join in the worship if they're familiar with the usual sequence of events. The aim of a liturgy is not to draw attention to itself but to God, to whom all our worship must be directed. A service which emphasises its own beauty is as self-defeating as one that seems chaotic. The shape of the liturgy should be such that worshippers don't notice it for itself, but through it are drawn closer to the living God, through Jesus his Son.

To whom should the service be directed?
'Family Service' shouldn't be a euphemism for 'children's service'. There's a valid and important place for the latter, but families consist of adults as well as children. If the whole service is made up of songs suitable for under-7s, and the sermon geared to the pre-school age-group, the rest of the congregation will feel left out or patronised (not without reason!). At the same time, those of riper years will need to allow for the presence of children. A sermon that's full of theological jargon will fly over the heads of anyone who hasn't got a theology degree; hymns with incomprehensible words and dreary tunes will bore most children to tears.

Children make a unique contribution to worship and to church life – they're not just the church of tomorrow, but the church of today. Adults can learn as much from them as we expect them to learn from us. Pitching the service at the right level is therefore a skill that takes time to develop. Those who seem to do it with least effort are probably those who work hardest at it! A service which is genuinely suited to all ages will be simple but not shallow, easy to assimilate but not superficial, enjoyable but not trivial.

What should the service contain?
Every act of worship should contain the reading of Scripture, and prayers of confession and intercession. Most worshippers would want to add music in the form of hymns (even in spoken services psalms and canticles are said by minister and congregation). The Church has always included a time when the Bible can be explained and the congregation exhorted (politely known as the 'sermon slot'). Other possible inclusions might be a Creed or Affirmation of Faith, spoken words of praise, a Baptism or the Eucharist. It is also good from time to time to allow certain groups to prepare and present a dramatic sketch to illustrate the theme, or a musical item suitable to the rest of the service. No one item should take too long, nor should any one element or person dominate the proceedings unduly. Not everything can be included in one service (though regrettably too many ministers try to!)

and the contents need to be reviewed critically beforehand to ensure continuity and brevity. So long as the service has a clear theme all material to be included can be tested against it and anything superfluous or distracting discarded. There are few more embarrassing sights than a congregation fidgeting and looking at their watches anxiously, while the service meanders on with no clear end in sight. Length and verbosity aren't spiritual virtues. On the contrary, they usually constitute a major obstacle to worship and spiritual growth.

All-age worship can fall into other traps. Sometimes it becomes a form of education, so that any material not deemed appropriate to improving spiritual understanding is omitted. There's no need to explain everything that's going to happen before it does. The aim of any act of worship is to give praise and glory to God, not to educate the congregation. It's often a source of amazement how much is taken in without any explanation, even by a small child. In fact, a 'liturgical compere' who overdoes the clarifying will probably end up leaving everyone in the dark. Good liturgy is self-explanatory.

Another error of judgement is to assume that those present are inclined either to be wholly traditionalist or totally trendy. There will always be a few with very decided opinions, but for the most part worshippers are fairly open to both ancient and modern. They certainly need one or two familiar landmarks, but around these can be placed contemporary hymns and worship songs, different forms of prayer, or a short drama. Liturgy has to relate to the culture in which it exists, so archaism for its own sake

(which has been described as the 'English Heritage' approach to worship) will soon drive people away. However, 'modern' has been defined as 'a word which describes something with no other virtue'. If everything is new and different, those who aren't familiar with church (and even some of those who are) will find the service hard to relate to. A sensible blend of the familiar and the contemporary helps to highlight the meaning of the former, and make the latter more attractive.

Perhaps the worst mistake is to equate 'spontaneity' with sloppiness. There's a right place for a spontaneous reaction to the work of the Holy Spirit – maybe by singing a different hymn or incorporating a brief silence or an extra prayer. It's sometimes desirable to allow off-the-cuff contributions from the congregation, perhaps during the intercessions. This is not an excuse for inadequate planning or preparation, however. A preacher once forgot his notes, so on entering the pulpit he apologised to his hearers. "I'm afraid my sermon notes are still on my desk at home" he said, with a red face, "so this morning you'll just have to listen to what the Holy Spirit gives me. Don't worry, it'll be the usual standard tonight!" Anyone who has a natural gift for speaking without notes in a spontaneous way will tell you how much hard work goes into preparing for it. The same is true of conducting a service. If there's an established pattern it's much easier to depart from it for a few moments without losing grip. It's not remotely honouring to God if no-one's sure what's going to happen next or who's responsible for it. Time is wasted, tempers get frayed among the ministers and the congregation is embarrassed. Worst of all, nobody has been drawn into worship or a deeper relationship with their heavenly Father. If we're to give God what he's worth to us, we should be content with nothing short of the highest possible standards in our worship.

Music

If there's one thing guaranteed to arouse everyone's passions after a service, then the music has no competitors! There can't be a vicar or minister in the land whose choice of hymns doesn't irritate somebody. "What made him choose that dreadful dirge?"; "Why can't we sing something we all know?"; "We'll have guitars in this church over my dead body!". Every church has its own distinctive tradition, be it high choral or charismatic band. We should be grateful to God for this rich diversity. However, whether it's English Hymnal or Graham Kendrick, hymns need to be well played and singable. For many people, the first and most abiding impression of a church service is the music. There are few wetter blankets to throw over worship than poorly played and drearily sung hymns. All-age worship encourages the congregation to take part and be involved in the liturgy. An out-of-tune piano, wheezy old organ or choir that's seen better days tends to have the opposite effect. At the other end of the scale a very formal service with magnificent music will do the same, as the fine musicianship soars above many worshippers' comprehension levels. Those who attend such a service from choice will enjoy it as they sit and listen – a valid act of worship, but hardly suitable for all ages.

One school of thought about music for all-age worship suggests that every hymn should be well-known and familiar. There's some point in this – people will obviously sing with more confidence if they know the tune. But what is well-known? Only a very small handful of hymns are well-known to everyone, churchgoers or not. To a large extent each congregation determines what is familiar, which in turn depends on its tradition, the hymn-book in use and musical resources available. So long as the musicians are confident, be they instrumentalists or vocalists, they can teach a congregation new material with little difficulty or complaint.

Another approach is to aim for the younger folk and fill the service with more modern hymns and songs. The advantage of this is that children and teenagers will be familiar with the style and idiom of the music, and may know some of the material from school. With a good worship group this can be spectacularly successful and create a tremendous impact. However, if it's not done confidently and well there will be a large-scale flop! There's also the disadvantage that older folk may feel alienated and ignored.

It would be sad if children grew up not having learned some of the great hymns of the past. There's no reason why they should enjoy them any less. The value of the material doesn't depend on the date it was first written. We're usually quite happy for children to enjoy the latest rock stars and groups, but we wouldn't want them to reject Beethoven and Chopin. Since the nineteenth and twentieth centuries aren't mutually exclusive they can easily come to appreciate both.

A blend of old and new is the ideal (the Church has usually adopted this approach throughout its history). It's a good move to start off with a hymn which will be readily recognised by everyone. The final hymn is also important, and at the very least should have a rousing and easily sung tune. As a general rule it's best to have no more than one new item in any one service, which should then be reinforced at regular intervals until it's 'one we all know'. It's also quite acceptable to use organ, choir and music group in the same service, or even in the same hymn. This prevents any style or group from being regarded as preferable or superior.

Most important of all, the music should reflect and develop the theme of the service. The musicians aren't concert performers (at least, not during the worship!) and the hymns are not an end in themselves. Like everything else in the liturgy, the music's sole purpose is to enable worshippers to draw closer to God. Each section in this book has some suggested hymns and songs to suit the theme, though you can probably think of others! A hymn which uses words from one of the Scripture readings, or leads into prayer in a helpful way, can have a profound effect on those who sing it. If the music for all-age worship is prepared as thoroughly and prayerfully as the sermon or the intercessions, it's unlikely there'll be many complaints. If it's all thrown together the previous night, will it really be worthy of God?

Readings

The public reading of Scripture has always been basic to Christian worship. The tradition of two or three passages, drawn from Old and New Testaments and the Gospels, being read publicly, ensures that the congregation see the connections between the different parts of the Bible. Using the lectionary is a good way of covering the whole range of the Bible, rather than just the parts that seem easier. On the other hand, the teaching programme of the church may necessitate choosing readings which deal with a particular theme. In any event, the reading of the Bible shouldn't be 'the mental cigarette break' between the Confession and the next hymn. If it's to be heard as God's Word by those listening it must be properly prepared and read with understanding. However, there's scope for imagination, too. Newcomers often find this an ideal way to become involved in the church's ministry and worship. Children can be integrated into the life of the fellowship by sharing in this part of the worship. Sometimes it's possible to typecast readers. I well remember a Mum-to-be reading the story of the Annunciation with an understanding not possible from anyone else. Other ideas might include mother and daughter reading on Mothering Sunday, or someone disabled reading about the gifts of the Holy Spirit.

Dramatised readings are excellent, too, and have a great impact when done well. Passages which involve dialogue are well-suited to this (eg some of Jesus' parables) but so too are passages from the prophets and even sections of Paul's letters. The most important element in the reading of Scripture is that it should be allowed to speak for itself. However it's read, and whoever reads it, the Bible is God's Word and deserves a central position in the service.

Ideally, readings shouldn't be overlong, but neither should they be too short and lose their context. Some narrative passages may need to take a little longer to cover the whole account, while parts of Paul's letters can seem very involved if too much is read. Suggestions are included, though by definition these can't be exhaustive. It's fruitless arguing over the best translation of the Bible, as there are so many opinions on this. Most churches have a preferred version and if everyone's familiar with it, there's no need to use anything else. Personally I prefer a modern translation which can be understood by those who don't come to church regularly, but I haven't yet found one that's perfect!

Prayers

In many respects the prayers of intercession are the most difficult part of a service to integrate into the whole. Whoever leads them needs to be sensitive to the 'mood' of the worship and somehow express in words what everyone else is thinking and praying. No easy task! Responsive prayers are useful in a number of ways. Many members of the congregation like to have something written down if they are to lead the intercessions, and feel a bit nervous at making up their own wording. The congregation feel more involved when they respond at certain points. If the same voice speaks for too long while everyone's eyelids are closed, some eyes may take longer than intended to reopen! Unfortunately, not all responsive prayers adapt easily to accommodate local needs, and there will be many who want to hear a public prayer for Mrs Jones in hospital, or the recently widowed Mr Smith. Often, too, events around the world will be high on the corporate agenda, though care is needed to avoid turning the prayers into a reading from the Guardian or Daily Telegraph. A variety of approaches always enriches the prayer life of a congregation, and the suggestions in this book give a flavour of the range of possibilities.

Brevity is vital. God doesn't need reminding about what's going on in the world, nor does he lack in understanding of theology! Too much material washes over those listening and fails to register. Simple, short prayers are the ideal, whatever the format. Children are usually capable of touching depths in one simple prayer which adult verbosity wouldn't approach, precisely because they don't become complicated by other issues. God doesn't value our prayers more because they're longer, or use longer words. On the contrary, wordiness is normally a block to our relationship with God. The late David Watson, while he was Rector of St Michael-le-Belfry, in York, once pointed to the Lord's Prayer, painted centuries earlier on one of the walls. The artist had run out of space for the first line, with the result that it read 'Our Father in Heaven, Hallo-'. As he remarked, the essence of prayer is contained in those five words.

Every act of worship should contain a Confession, when together God's people recognise their own sinfulness and failings and come before him to acknowledge this and receive his forgiveness. We're only worthy to come into God's presence because of Jesus' death and resurrection. However, the emphasis in Confession is not our wrongdoing but God's mercy and grace. This book includes a Confession and Absolution for each theme, though some are interchangeable. As with the intercessions there are corporate biddings and responsive prayers, so that the congregation doesn't become too familiar with the same wording or style.

The Sermon

A wise preacher once said: "To preach for an hour would take an hour's preparation. To preach for half-an-hour would take me half a day to prepare. To preach for five minutes I'd probably need a week!" The sermon or address is perhaps the focal point of an all-age service, because it draws together the different strands of the theme and explains them. There are two dangers – aiming at adults, and aiming at children! If you speak solely to the grown-ups, the kids will soon get restive and bored, but if you pitch it at the six-year-olds, everyone else will feel it's beneath them and switch off. Visual aids, even of the simplest kind, are a huge asset, provided they don't take over. I heard of a preacher who once ate a daffodil as part of his address – it was very memorable, but no-one could remember what it was about!

If you don't feel too confident about addressing all ages at once, or handling visual aids, don't despair. Every theme has a suggested sermon with suitable illustrations. If you're one of the few who find it easy, beware! The sermon can easily degenerate into a liturgical cabaret act, and too much patter soon doubles the length. However 'off-the-cuff' some people can appear to be in their delivery, the spontaneity has almost certainly been well-prepared and rehearsed. The sermon also has to fit into the rest of the liturgy, and while

it is of necessity the focal point, it shouldn't overwhelm the other components, but lead naturally from them and into them.

The Eucharist

Whatever your tradition calls it, the consecration and distribution of the bread and wine will inevitably be the climax of the liturgy if it's included. The whole service is geared to it and looks forward to it. An all-age Eucharist is a powerful symbol of the unifying love of Jesus, as all are drawn to him, whatever their age, gender, race, background or education. In him we are made one, and all other distinctions fade into insignificance as we join together to receive forgiveness, new life and the strength of his Holy Spirit. Every church will have its own sacramental traditions and emphases, and it would be wrong to single out any particular approach as superior. However, mystery and approachability aren't mutually exclusive. Some occasions, such as Christmas, Easter, Harvest and Pentecost are particularly suited to an all-age Family Communion service. It's good to encourage everyone to come to the altar-rail, either to receive bread and wine or a blessing. Many folk who don't wish to take the sacrament prefer to kneel at the altar-rail for a blessing rather than remain in their seats, and often whole families come up together. Some people find that the unavoidable noise of children at this part of the service is too distracting, but provided there are other services which cater for them, I would want to encourage children not to view the altar as somewhere grown-up and out of bounds, but as a place where they too can meet with their heavenly

Father and enjoy his blessings. They also soon learn that it's best to be quiet there.

Other Elements

There are many other possibilities for inclusion in all-age worship. Sometimes it's helpful to incorporate an Affirmation of Faith appropriate to the occasion. Spoken words of praise are also an asset, as is a spoken Psalm. Given the necessary resources, drama and dance can powerfully underline the theme of the service – there are many books of sketches and short dramas for use in churches. This really needs a great deal of practice beforehand, as anything substandard will be measured against the standards now set by television.

A Baptism also fits wonderfully into an all-age service, especially if the family concerned are part of the church fellowship. It even includes its own affirmation of faith! There are alternative words for the Peace, for the prayers after Communion, and for the Blessing. There's no reason why any act of worship should become dreary or dull, given the variety of material now available.

Service Sheets

Increasing numbers of churches now own or hire a photocopier, and few if any have no access to one. A service sheet can be a great help, especially if it includes all the words needed by the congregation, plus an outline of the shape of the service. Those not so accustomed to church may be daunted by the size of the books they're given, or get lost after five minutes because they aren't sure about the page number. If you produce a special service sheet, make sure that it's neatly laid out and comprehensible. A scruffy piece of paper which makes little sense is worse than nothing and downgrades the whole act of worship. Everything about our worship should be of the highest possible standard – occasional mistakes are unavoidable, but sloppiness isn't! The aim is not to be 'professional' or slick, nor to impress all newcomers with the standard attained, but to bring glory to God. We owe him the very best we can give.

The Old Testament

The Old Testament is full of wonderful characters and exciting narratives. I've selected five of the best-known figures, but there are many more. Some of the suggested readings are inevitably quite long; you may want to cut them down, though small chunks of a narrative account may have little meaning out of context. The possibilities for dramatised readings are legion.

The ideas for all-age addresses are only outlines. It's assumed that the points will be fleshed out with illustrations from the life of the character concerned. It's good, too, to draw out the parallels with the New Testament as well as the applications to our own Christian lives.

Abraham – Mr Faith

Abraham sums up Israel's relationship with God. They looked back to him as Mr Faith. He was their founding father, the prototype of what God was calling his people to be. When Jesus wanted to demonstrate who he was to the religious leaders he said, "Before Abraham was, I am," a statement which was considered blasphemous. Paul used Abraham as his example when writing to the early churches about what it means to have faith in God. Abraham was willing to leave everything he knew in the city of Ur to obey the call of God. He left behind his friends and security to set out for a country he'd never seen, not knowing when he'd get there, or what difficulties he'd meet on the way. He trusted God to keep his promise that he would one day become the father of a great nation, even though Sarah his wife wasn't able to bear children. Later he had faith that God knew what he was doing, despite being told by him to kill his only son. When Lot chose the 'soft option' and left Abraham to the more rugged hill country, it didn't worry him; he trusted God to protect and bless him in any circumstances. There are many incidents in Abraham's life which can teach us about faith in God. It's possible to focus on one of these, or alternatively to look at how Abraham exercised faith in these various episodes. In either event the emphasis is on our relationship with God and how that affects our life here on earth.

READINGS
Genesis 12:1–9/13:1–12 (or 18)/17:1–8, 15–22/18:1–15/22:1–14/Psalm 105:1–11/ Romans 4:13–25/Galatians 3:6–14/ Hebrews 11:8–12/John 8:31–41

HYMNS
Traditional
The God of Abraham praise
Guide me, O thou great Jehovah
He who would valiant be
Have faith in God, my heart
Forth in thy name

Modern
Be bold, be strong
Praise the name of Jesus
Living under the shadow
I want to walk with Jesus Christ
Send me out from here, Lord

CONFESSION
Heavenly Father, you call us to follow you in faith, as you did your servant Abraham. We are sorry that we fail to put our trust in you, looking instead to the world around. Forgive our lack of faith and grant us the vision to see that your way is best, through Christ our Lord, Amen.

Almighty God, who forgives all who come to him in repentance and faith, have mercy upon you, pardon and deliver you from all your sins, confirm and strengthen you in all goodness and keep you in everlasting life, for the sake of Jesus Christ our Lord, Amen.

INTERCESSION
We kneel before the Lord who calls us to follow him, saying:
Faithful Lord,
Receive our prayers.

Lord God, you call your Church to bear witness to your love as revealed to us in Christ your Son. Give strength to all who serve your Kingdom in worship, leadership, teaching and service. Especially we pray for the

Church in ... May they know your
power and love as they seek to fulfil
what you have called them to do.
Faithful Lord,
Receive our prayers.

Lord God, you call your people to live
in this world by faith. Give strength to
all entrusted with positions of
authority and influence, that they may
lead the nations in righteousness and
justice. Especially we pray ...
Faithful Lord,
Receive our prayers.

Lord God, you call us to follow you in
times of joy and sadness. Give
strength to anyone known to us who is
anxious or sad, lonely or distressed,
and finding it hard to keep you in
view. Especially we pray for ... May
they know your comfort and peace as
they hold on to your promises.
Faithful Lord,
**Receive our prayers. May we not only
hear your call but answer it as we
serve you in our church, our
community and among our friends,
for the sake of your Son Jesus Christ
who obeyed you even to the Cross.
Amen.**

ALL-AGE ADDRESS
Faith isn't the easiest concept to convey. As James pointed out in his letter
to early Christians, it's seen far more
in actions than understood from
words. A great deal of faith may be
needed to use this idea! Before the
service, hide two £1 coins somewhere
in the church building, as far as possible from where you're speaking, without losing sight of it. Ask a boy and a
girl to come up, and then place a
blindfold on each of them (this isn't
ageism – adults don't usually like

volunteering to do such things!).
When you're sure they can't see, point
them in the same direction and start to
give them instructions as to where to
go. From experience this needs a fair
amount of detail (eg 'six paces forwards, then turn to your right').
Sooner or later they'll find the coin, or
whatever treasure you've hidden.

The points are clear enough. The
two guinea-pigs have to put their trust
in you for several reasons:
i) they can't be certain that you've
really hidden something for them to
find,
ii) they only have your word for it
that you're sending them the right
way,
iii) they need to follow your instructions precisely,
iv) they have to believe the prize is
theirs to keep (which may determine
what kind of 'treasure' you use!).

Overall, they have to be confident
that you mean what you say, otherwise they may give up or try to make
their own way. All of these were true
of Abraham. He had no idea where
God was sending him, or what he'd
find when he arrived there. He knew
he had to trust God's instructions and
obey them. He did it because he
believed God would reward him. The
same is true for all Christians as they
live the Christian life and exercise
their faith.

Jacob – Mr Nasty

If Abraham was Israel's Mr Faith, then Jacob has to be Mr Nasty. He was devious, vindictive and rather cowardly. Smooth and charming on the surface, he was cunning and manipulative underneath. Are we really talking about one of the three great founding fathers of Israel, God's special people? The Bible never disguises the faults of even its great characters, and by any standards Jacob seems very unlikely material for God to use. He was the stop-at-home, unlike his older brother Esau, who was the outdoor, physical type. He was strongly influenced by his mother Rebecca, and certainly had no qualms about taking advantage of his ageing father's blindness to steal the birthright from Esau, to whom it properly belonged. Yet when he was found out he soon ran away from the situation. He got his come-uppance from the equally deceitful Laban, and ended up with a wife he wasn't expecting, so he crossed black and white sheep to pay his uncle back.

Yet in the midst of all this he had two life-changing encounters with God. One was at Bethel, where he dreamt of a ladder between Heaven and earth. The other was at Peniel, where he wrestled with God. Only after this does he put matters right with his older brother and commit himself wholly to following God.

Jacob is a wonderful example of how God can call and use the most unpromising people to serve him. If Abraham is a picture of living by faith, Jacob's pilgrimage demonstrates how God never gives up on us, but transforms us as we encounter him on our journey through life. Interestingly, we're as aware of Jacob in his old age as we are of his youthful escapades, an elderly man who looks back and recognises that 'God has been my shepherd all my life to this day'. I wonder if when he

first ran away from Esau's anger, Jacob could have foreseen how one day he would end up blessing twelve sons, even the one he thought was dead. That's how far God brought him!

READINGS
Genesis 27:1–40 (19–35)/28:10–22/31:1–13/32:1–12/32:22–30/35:1–7/45:25–46:4/Psalm 40:1–8/2 Corinthians 4:7–18/Hebrews 11:13–21/John 4:4–14

HYMNS
Traditional
O God of Bethel by whose hand
O for a closer walk with God
Just as I am
Be thou my vision
Children of the heavenly king

Modern
Jesus, take me as I am
We shall stand
Father, I place into your hands
Change my heart, O God
Jesus, you are changing me

CONFESSION
Lord God, we acknowledge before you our many sins and failures, and repent of all our wrong attitudes and actions. Cleanse us from everything which spoils our relationship with you, and fill us afresh with the life-changing power of the Holy Spirit of Jesus, our Saviour and Lord. Amen.

God our Heavenly Father, who accepts and forgives all who turn to him in repentance, grant unto you pardon for all your sins, peace in your heart, and confidence in his guiding hand, through Jesus Christ our Lord. Amen.

INTERCESSION

We come before our Heavenly King as his children, in whose prayers he delights, saying:
Father, uphold us,
Strengthen and guide us.

We ask you to bless all who with us are members of your family here on earth. Assure them of your love and direction, and give them strength to fulfil your calling. We pray today for ... May they know your joy and peace as they faithfully serve you.
Father, uphold them,
Strengthen and guide them.

We ask you to bless all who have authority over us and influence the running of society. Give them a clear understanding of your standards and concerns, and a vision of your will for this world. We pray today ... May your kingdom come on earth as in Heaven.
Father, uphold them,
Strengthen and guide them.

We ask you to bless all who are suffering through illness, sadness or anxiety, especially those known to us. Assure them of your eternal presence and give them courage to face their situation. We pray today for ... May they receive your comfort in this time of difficulty and grief.
Father, uphold them,
Strengthen and guide them.

We ask you to bless us as we continue our earthly pilgrimage towards your eternal kingdom. Give us a sure foundation for faith and hope for the future and keep us true to our calling in Christ Jesus.
Father, uphold us,
Strengthen and guide us, until we reach our goal to live with you for ever through Jesus Christ our Saviour, Amen.

ALL-AGE ADDRESS

This particular address focuses on God taking hold of Jacob's life and transforming it. It needs a little preparation, and some protection for clothes or robes may prove useful. Begin by asking one or two people in the congregation what their favourite food is. Most will choose something fairly predictable, though one or two might opt for curry or frogs' legs! Bring out a bag of flour and ask if anyone would like to taste it – whether or not someone takes the offer up, tip some into a large bowl or container. Repeat this procedure with butter, sugar and milk, so that they're all thrown in together. If at this point you add some salt there are sure to be a few grimaces! Offer the mixture around and ask why people are turning it down.

The ingredients are all edible, but look distinctly unappetising. Something needs to happen before we'll eat it. Bring out some scones which have been baked previously and point out that although the ingredients are identical, the difference lies in what's happened to them in the oven.

The ingredients of Jacob's life must have looked a terrible mess at some points, but God took them and in meeting with him at Bethel and Peniel changed them into someone who would follow him and do his will. As we meet with him, God can take even the worst messes we feel we've made of our lives and turn them into something he can use. Stress that no-one is so bad that God can't change them. Jacob used to be deceitful, cowardly and manipulative, always looking to get his own way. If God could use him, he can use anybody.

Joseph – Mr Special

Whether or not the Israelites saw Joseph as Mr Special is open to debate. Outside the book of Genesis, he's mentioned rather less often than Abraham, Isaac and Jacob, and in the New Testament hardly at all. But he certainly saw himself as Mr Special, a view encouraged by his father. Joseph was Rachel's first son, and no doubt Jacob treasured this association with his favourite wife. Unfortunately his older brothers weren't of the same opinion. Thanks to Messrs Lloyd Webber and Rice, the story of Joseph and his amazing technicolour dreamcoat is one of the best-known of Old Testament stories (deservedly so, for it makes a gripping narrative). At the same time, the stage production hardly mentions God, though when Joseph reveals his identity to his brothers, he says "It wasn't you who sent me here, but God".

Like most spoiled children Joseph had become rather prissy and self-righteous, unable to see his own faults and failings but intensely aware of the shortcomings of others. He had a strong sense of his destiny, which must have been sorely tried during his slavery and captivity. His confidence in God grew, however, and he was not afraid to stand up for what was right, nor later in prison to relay accurately what God had said. Even after a few years in prison, Joseph still had confidence that one day he'd be vindicated by God.

Like Joseph, we can trust God to protect and lead us, even when everything's going wrong. Under considerable provocation in Potiphar's house, Joseph refused to give in to temptation, but obeyed God. Like his father, he could look back at the end of his life and see that his faith wasn't misplaced. He was special in God's plan – and so are we.

Readings

Genesis 37:2–36/39:1–45:28 (any section of this will do)/Psalm 40:1–10/ Psalm 105:8–22/Acts 7:9–15/ 2 Corinthians 6:3–10/Matthew 6:25–34

Hymns

Traditional

Through the night of doubt and sorrow
Through all the changing scenes
Oft in danger, oft in woe
Stand up, stand up for Jesus
God is working his purpose out

Modern

Thanks be to God who gives
Rejoice, rejoice, Christ is in you
He that is in us
Let God arise
You are my hiding place

Confession

Heavenly Father, we come before you, knowing that we have not always put our trust in you. We are sorry for allowing the crises of this life to weaken our faith. Forgive our sins and failings, we pray, and restore us to your glorious presence through your Son, Jesus Christ our Lord, Amen.

God our Father, who never lets go of his children, grant you pardon for all your sins, faith to accept his perfect plan, and the peace of his Son Jesus Christ our Lord, Amen.

Intercession

Confident that he will hear and answer us, we pray to our loving Father, saying:
Lord of all,
Help us to trust you.

Loving Father, so many things happen in our world which distress us. We pray today for . . . Be with those who suffer from violence, fear or exploitation. May they know you near them, protecting them and giving them peace.
Lord of all,
Help them to trust you.

Loving Father, so many people in our world need to hear the good news of your Kingdom. We pray today for . . . Be with all who are homeless, unemployed, or deprived. May they know your care and comfort and turn to you in their need.
Lord of all,
Help them to trust you.

Loving Father, so many parts of our world need the government of the Prince of Peace. We pray today for . . . Be with those who govern us and influence the affairs of the nations. May they know your guiding hand directing them in the paths of righteousness.
Lord of all,
Help them to trust you.

Loving Father, so many known to us need your healing touch on their lives. We pray today for . . . Be with them in sorrow, anxiety, ill health or adversity. May they feel your arms of love embracing them and upholding them.
Lord of all,
Help them to trust you.

Loving Father, we too need your presence every day. Be with us wherever we go and in whatever we do. May we follow you more closely and grow in faith for the sake of your Son, our Saviour Jesus Christ, Amen.

ALL-AGE ADDRESS
This idea is a variant on the one used for illustrating faith in the section on Abraham. It may be best not to have these two addresses close together! The main similarity is in using two blindfolds, preferably on children who won't be embarrassed! Before the service, establish three or four 'obstacles', such as a rope between pews, a pile of old hymnbooks or a beanbag. However, make sure they aren't an obstacle to the rest of the congregation. Each obstacle can represent one of the hurdles we face in life – crisis, bereavement, illness, unemployment, death etc. Three or four are adequate to make the point. As well as those who are blindfolded, you'll need two volunteer 'guides' to steer them around or across the obstacles. If each obstacle is labelled, this can be read out and explained. A 'destination' should also be established. The confidence that's needed in the two guides is considerable. When they've completed the course, demonstrate how Joseph had that kind of confidence in God. Despite many difficulties and disasters his faith didn't waver. He knew God would get him to where he should be. Many find the concept of trusting God very hard to put into practice in daily living. Give some examples therefore, either of individuals who've trusted God in a time of trial and experienced his guidance, or of situations in which we might have to trust him in that way.

Moses – Mr Obedient

Moses can sometimes seem a rather stern and forbidding character. It's easier in some ways to relate to the patriarchs, with all their faults. Perhaps it's because Moses is so associated with The Law of God, that he comes across like a reproving JP. He had a central role in God's plan for his people, and is remembered no less today than in past centuries for bringing the Israelites out of Egypt into the Promised Land. He was also very human! We see him seething with anger, whether at the cruelty of an Egyptian slave driver or at the stubborn whining of God's people in the desert. Maybe we identify with him most in his lack of confidence. Moses took a great deal of convincing by God that he was the one to take the people out of slavery. Full of excuses, you get the impression that nothing would have suited Moses better than a quiet life in the country! He was plagued with self-doubt and a low self-esteem. As usual, one of the pivotal figures in God's dealings with his people was from a human viewpoint quite unsuited to the task. Moses also highlights the need for obedience to God's law. Obedience was part of the Covenant relationship, albeit one that proved impossible to adhere to. As Paul explains, keeping the rules isn't an alternative to living by faith, but a demonstration of our love for God and commitment to him. Indeed, we shouldn't look at the commandments as rules at all, but as a reflection of God's character, with which we seek to identify. In tackling the theme of obedience, there's always the risk of moralising creeping in. The British sense of 'duty' is sometimes a hindrance to understanding what it means. God has given us a framework within which we can conduct our lives. It's a bit like a football pitch – without it, the game will soon end in chaos! James calls it 'the perfect law which gives freedom'.

READINGS
Exodus 3:1–10/7–15/4:1–17/6:28–7:13/
8:20–32/10:1–20/12:1–13/29–39/
14:15–31/17:1–7/20:1–21/32:15–26/
34:1–10/Numbers 21:4–9/Psalm 119:9–
16/97–104/Acts 7:30–39/2 Corinthians
3:7–18/Hebrews 3:1–6/John 3:1–15/
7:14–24

HYMNS
Traditional
Guide me, O thou great Jehovah
All my hope on God is founded
Lord, enthroned in heavenly splendour
Father, hear the prayer we offer
Bread of Heaven

Modern
I want to walk with Jesus Christ
Reign in me
The Lord has led forth his people
We are marching
We are a chosen people

CONFESSION
Almighty God, your word is for all time and your commandments are for all people. We confess that we have not listened to your voice and failed to obey your laws. Forgive our disobedience and self-will. Give us grace to follow your instruction and walk with you in faith, through your Son Jesus Christ our Lord, Amen.

God our merciful Father, who accepts all who return to him, grant you forgiveness for all your wrongdoing, time for amendment of life, and the grace of his Holy Spirit now and always, through Christ our Saviour, Amen.

INTERCESSION
We approach our sovereign Lord with confidence that he will listen to our requests, saying:
Mighty Lord,
Help us to obey you.

King of the nations we bow before you. In your hands are the peoples of this world; kings and rulers acknowledge your authority. We pray for those who hold power . . . May they be humbled by your presence and obey your direction.
Mighty Lord,
Help them to obey you.

Lord of the Church, we kneel in worship. Your hand is upon those who accept you as Lord of their lives. We pray for all who hold office in the church, bishops and priests, lay leaders and members of councils . . . May they be filled with your Holy Spirit of wisdom and discernment as they lead your people in faith.
Mighty Lord,
Help them to obey you.

Ruler of our lives, we open ourselves to your work of grace in us. You dwell in the hearts of all who accept you, and bring your healing touch to the areas of pain and sadness. We pray today for . . . May they be touched by your love and experience the wholeness of your presence.
Mighty Lord,
Help them to obey you.

Sovereign Lord, we commit ourselves to serving you. May we be empowered to do your will and proclaim your works.
Mighty Lord,
Help us to obey you as we hear your

still small voice within, for the sake of your Son, our Saviour Jesus Christ, Amen.

ALL-AGE ADDRESS
Obedience can mean different things at different times. It's vital to underline the meaning of obedience in the Christian life, and one way of doing this is to demonstrate various types of obedience.

1) Simple obedience. Persuade two or three children to come forward and take part in a game of 'Simon says'. In this case they're being asked to obey a simple one-off instruction. God's law isn't one-off – it's for all time and all people.

2) Reluctant obedience. Ask a child to do something sensible, but which it might not enjoy. Washing hands is a good example (this may need adapting to local circumstances). Stress here that cleanliness is not just occasionally necessary, but a basic part of life. We may not feel inclined to keep certain laws, but they're necessary (eg keeping to the speed limit). God's laws are a necessary part of life.

3) Mindless obedience. Ask a child to do something really daft – like standing upside down in the pulpit and reciting the alphabet backwards. It's unlikely that you'll get immediate compliance! Point out that some governments may expect this kind of obedience from their subjects. God doesn't. He wants us to do his will because we know that it's the best way. He's given us a mind and expects us to use it.

4) Unselfish obedience. You could simply ask a volunteer to fetch you a

glass of water or similar. He or she will gain no personal benefit from doing as you request, except a thank you. God wants us to obey him like this, not because we'll get anything out of it (he gives us his blessings without any strings attached!) but simply because it pleases him. Explain how Jesus obeyed his heavenly Father unselfishly in going to the cross, so that we could be forgiven and enjoy new life in him for ever. God's law is never restrictive, but leads to the greatest freedom we can ever know.

David – Mr Nice

Abraham may be the most revered of the great figures of Israel's history, and Moses the most respected, but there can be little doubt that the most popular was David. The circumstances of his anointing as king were a bit unusual, but that never made any difference to his popularity rating. A talented musician and poet, a skilful warrior, a fine military strategist and a leader of genuine vision, David's reign was always held up as the ideal of what Israel could be. Under his rule the empire extended, enemies were defeated and prosperity grew. He seemed incapable of being disliked, and was often compared favourably to others, especially his predecessor, Saul. His life is a kaleidoscope of different events and incidents, so it's not easy to select one which sums him up. His bout with Goliath will be the first to enter most people's minds, and his affair with Bathsheba may well be the next, but neither are entirely satisfactory for use in all-age worship, and need very careful handling. David was a supremely self-confident individual, bolstered by his own success. This stood him in good stead when faced with Goliath, but turned into an illusion of infallibility when he was confronted by the beauties of Bathsheba. Such a nice man wouldn't kill his enemy, Saul; instead he wept over his death in battle. He wept too over the demise of his evil son Absalom.

His life wasn't by any means free of sadness or pain, yet David was victorious in the end, not only in battle, but in his leadership of the nation over forty years. In treating this as a theme, take care to avoid the equation of 'victorious Christian living' with 'being successful'. David was always first to acknowledge that all his victories were God-given and that any 'success' was entirely due to his trust in God. Indeed his biggest single failure came at a time when this lapsed, and he gave in to temptation. In many respects he was Israel's greatest king and deserved his great popularity and reputation, but this was the result of his close relationship with God. Even this 'friend of God' could get it all wrong when he became too full of himself!

READINGS
1 Samuel 16:1–13/17:20–50/20:18–42/24:1–22/26:5–24/2 Samuel 5:17–25/7:1–16/9/11:1–17/12:1–14/18:24–33/Psalm 3/4/6/9/13/18/20/23/27/30/32/34/37/40/51/57/63/122/139/145/Acts 2:22–36/13:16–26/1 Corinthians 15:50–58/Ephesians 6:10–20/1 John 5:1–5/Mark 12:35–40/Matthew 21:1–11

HYMNS
Traditional
We rest on Thee
Soldiers of Christ, arise
Thy hand, O God, has guided
Onward, Christian soldiers
Crown him with many crowns

Modern
In heavenly armour
Thanks be to God
Victory is on our lips
For this purpose
Show your power, O Lord

CONFESSION
Let us admit to God the sin which always confronts us.

Lord God,
we have done evil in your sight;
we have sinned against you alone.
We are sorry and repent.
Have mercy on us according to your love.
Wash away our wrong-doing and cleanse us from our sin.

Renew a right spirit within us
and restore us to the joy of your
salvation,
through Jesus Christ our Lord,
Amen.   *Psalm 51*

May the God of forgiveness
show you his mercy,
forgive you your sins,
and bring you to everlasting life,
through Jesus Christ our Lord, Amen.

INTERCESSION
We bring our prayers and requests
with thanksgiving to our victorious
Saviour, saying:
Jesus, in your Name,
Give us the victory.

Lord Jesus, on the cross you defeated
all the powers of evil and death. You
have opened for us the way to eternal
life. May we and all who own your
name rejoice in your victory and
experience it in our lives. We pray
especially for the church in . . . and for
this church . . . Jesus, in your name,
Give us the victory.

Lord Jesus, by your death you won for
us peace and assurance of the Father's
love. You bring peace to our troubled
hearts and needy world. May we and
all who rule the nations know that
perfect peace and seek to bring it to
those people and places torn apart by
violence and warfare. We pray
especially for . . .
Jesus, in your name,
Give us the victory.

Lord Jesus, by your mighty
resurrection you offer us forgiveness,
freedom from fear, and the hope of life
for evermore. You bring hope out of
our despair and joy out of our sorrow.

May all who are suffering from grief or
anxiety recognise your loving
presence. We pray especially for . . .
Jesus, in your name,
**Give us the victory. Help us to
recognise our weaknesses but trust in
your great strength and claim your
victory, in the all-conquering name of
your Son, our Saviour Jesus Christ,
Amen.**

ALL-AGE ADDRESS
The concept of victory is not easy to
put across using participants from the
congregation. Any kind of competition
could become prolonged, and if
there's too much excitement in the air
the point of the address will be lost!
For this idea you'll need either a flip-
chart or an overhead projector (and an
artist who can do simple cartoons if
you don't feel you have sufficient skill
in this department).

The first picture would be of a
sporting triumph – either by your local
football, rugby or cricket team, or by
the national side. Either the winning
goal or the trophy could be depicted.
Sports teams win because they have
greater skill or strength. They may go
to great lengths to find out about their
opponents. Although David was a
gifted military leader he knew that all
his victories came from God.

The second picture could be of a
mountaineer on top of a mountain
peak. We might say he'd overcome the
forces of nature, as well as his own
fears. It's very much his achievement.
David knew that everything he
achieved was due to God's goodness
and power working in him. Jesus
never exalted himself either, drawing
attention only to his Father in Heaven.

The third picture could be of any
army winning in battle. Point out that

not all wars are fought for good reasons, but sometimes they're necessary to defeat evil.

The triumphant army will bring the defeated one under its aegis. It can impose its laws and even its culture. There are good examples from recent history to illustrate this. David defeated other armies, often those of barbaric tribes around Israel. Jesus vanquished the forces of Satan, everything that is at enmity with God, by his death on the cross. Like David, he trusted his Father to give him the victory.

Our lives will have plenty of difficulties and crisis points, but we won't overcome them by being superstrong or clever, nor by great achievements. Only as we trust God's power and the victory he's already won will we come through them, recognising that human success counts for nothing in God's kingdom.

The Prophets

In some ways the Old Testament prophets can seem severe and daunting, yet their message is as relevant to the twentieth century as it was to those who first heard it. The prophetic books aren't always easy to understand, and some knowledge of the background history is needed to tease out their meaning. Yet it's possible to extract particular themes and emphases in a way that can be understood by anyone.

The readings are easier to keep short, and it's better if they don't become too long. Those selected are all fairly well-known, but other passages may also effectively underline the same issues. Above all, ensure that those listening understand the messages as God's word to us now. Times may change but people don't!

Elijah – God's Power

Elijah was the first of the great prophets. Israel had a long history of prophetic ministry but not all were reliable messengers of God. Elijah was the genuine article, unafraid of King Ahab and recognised as one of the most important figures in Israel's history – notice how he appears on the Mount of the Transfiguration. He was the representative of the prophets, as was Moses of The Law.

Yet strangely there are not many accounts of his ministry. The most famous narratives are the widow of Zarephath and the contest with the prophets of Baal on Mount Carmel.

The message of Elijah is summed up in those two dramatic incidents, which reveal to us how God's power can transform the life of an individual or a nation. The widow had experienced God's provision already in a time of famine, but only when her son was resuscitated did she truly accept the power of God in her situation. The people of Israel also needed God to deliver them, both from a lengthy drought and from a weak monarch dominated by a scheming and wicked wife. The confrontation on Mount Carmel is perhaps the most spectacular demonstration of God's power against that of other gods anywhere in the Old Testament. On both occasions Elijah did only one thing – he prayed. He's the epitome of the truth that all God's people need to learn, that only when we come to God in prayer, open ourselves to him, and allow him into a situation, do we see his power manifested. Israel had had plenty of evidence, but again they'd forgotten. We too need continual reminding that our God isn't remote, distant and uninvolved; if we let him he will show his power both in our own lives and to the whole of society.

READINGS
1 Kings 17:1–16/17–24/18:16–46 (or 25–39)/Psalm 66/68/145/147/Acts 1:1–11/4:23–31/Romans 15:13–20/Ephesians 3:14–21/Luke 5:17–26/John 11:32–45

HYMNS
Traditional
I sing the almighty power of God
All hail the power of Jesus' name
O worship the King
Come let us join our cheerful songs
Lord of all power, I give you my will

Modern
Jesus is Lord!
Show your power, O Lord
O Lord our God (we will magnify)
I will give thanks
Jesus shall take the highest honour

CONFESSION
We confess our sins to Almighty God, saying:
Lord of love,
Forgive and restore us.

We are sorry for the times when we have gone our own way and not put our trust in your mighty power.
Lord of love,
Forgive and restore us.

We are sorry for the times when we have not opened our hearts to your saving power, trusting instead in our own righteousness.
Lord of love,
Forgive and restore us.

We are sorry for the times when we have doubted your transforming power, allowing despair to rule our hearts.
Lord of love,
Forgive and restore us.

We are sorry for the times when your power has not been seen in our lives. Lord of love,
Forgive and restore us so that we will be worthy servants and true channels of your power in the world, through Jesus Christ our Lord, Amen.

INTERCESSION
Heavenly Father, all power belongs to you. The world was created and sustained by your mighty word. Mankind has been redeemed and brought back to you by your mighty salvation. Your people are strengthened and enabled by your all-powerful Spirit. May we be channels of that power to those around us, revealing you in all your glory as sovereign of the whole universe, our Saviour Jesus Christ, Amen.

Almighty God, we ask that your power will be seen in our world today. Break into the areas of pain and darkness and shed your glorious light . . . Break into the life of your Church, destroying apathy and fear and awakening your people to proclaim the good news of your saving love . . . Break into the lives of all who are in sadness, distress or anxiety, especially . . . Break into our lives by the power of your Holy Spirit, removing all that would hinder our witness and filling us with boldness to bear witness to your love in word and deed. This we ask in the mighty name of Jesus our Lord, Amen.

ALL-AGE ADDRESS
As with other aspects of God's character, his power requires careful explanation if misunderstandings are to be avoided. Even today many will think of this as something mystical or magical, turning God into a celestial conjuror. To have God's power within us certainly doesn't mean we can automatically do the impossible! Power is most evident from its effects – Ian Botham's batting, Nigel Mansell's car or whatever example you take.

One of the best illustrations of the Christian concept of God's power is electricity. Three different appliances are used for this talk: a radio or cassette player, a lamp and a tool (such as a vacuum cleaner, food mixer or typewriter). None of them have any power of their own. Without electricity they're useless. They need to be connected to the source of the power at the socket. Only when that power is constantly flowing into them do they function as they're meant to, giving information, illumination and help.

Demonstrate each appliance, using the parallel with God's power. He helps us to speak in the right way at the right time, especially to share his good news with others. He helps us to see better, in the sense of understanding. And he helps us to serve him better and live for other people as Jesus did. God's power in our lives isn't an impersonal, incomprehensible force. God fills us with his Holy Spirit, so that we don't try to live in our own strength. That's why Elijah just prayed – he knew he could do nothing on his own. God's power needs to be flowing into us all the time, in every moment of our lives if we're to be effective for his Kingdom.

Isaiah – God's Call

There's a fair chance that in an average congregation (if there is such a thing), the best-known prophet will be Isaiah. That's not to say that everyone will be familiar with the character, but his words are among the best-loved in the whole Bible. Handel's Messiah has imprinted 'Comfort ye' (to take just one example) on the minds of many who'd never enter a church for worship, even if they aren't sure where the words come from.

Isaiah, however, is a difficult book. It's an interesting theological issue, but most all-age services won't improve for an exposition of the arguments about how many Isaiahs there were. Modern scholarship seems to be fairly clear that chapters 40–66 date from the latter years of the Babylonian exile, while the first 39 are from the time of the Assyrian threat, some one hundred and fifty years earlier. It's probably best not to mix these two parts in one talk, in order to avoid confusion. God's message is the same, whatever the historical background. Many themes can be found in this, the longest of the prophetic books, but the one that many will remember is Isaiah's call in chapter 6. It's the most detailed account in the Bible of someone being called to serve God, and speaks volumes to us about how the Lord commissions us into his service.

If there's a preference for using the latter part of Isaiah, the overriding theme is God breaking into captivity and despair and promising a new start. This theme is parallel to the one taken from Jeremiah in the next section and some of that material would be suitable.

READINGS

Isaiah 6:1–8/42:1–4/49:1–7/Psalm 65/
105:37–45/132:11–18/Acts 9:1–19/
Romans 8:28–39/1 Peter 2:4–9/
Matthew 4:18–22/John 1:35–51/15:9–17

HYMNS
Traditional
Jesus calls us
O thou who camest from above
O Jesus, I have promised
Dear Lord and Father of mankind
My God, how wonderful thou art

Modern
Abba Father
I want to serve the purpose of God
Open our eyes, Lord
Lord come and heal your church
You are the vine

CONFESSION
Mighty Lord, you are the Holy One, glorious in majesty, awesome in power. We see you reigning in splendour, King of all. But our lips are unclean, our hands stained. Cleanse us from our guilt, we pray, and forgive our sinfulness. Make us worthy to stand in your presence and serve you through the merits of our Saviour Jesus Christ, Amen.

Almighty God, whose mercy is without limit, pardon and deliver you from all your sins, take away your guilt and make you fit to do his will for the sake of him who calls us, Jesus Christ our Lord, Amen.

INTERCESSION
We enter the presence of the King of Kings, saying:
Holy Lord, hear our cry,
And make us more like you.

Lord God, your thoughts are higher than ours. We cannot take in your greatness, yet we can know your love. Give to your church a fresh vision of

your holiness and your grace, and inspire her to make your glory known throughout the world . . .
Holy Lord, hear our cry,
And make us more like you.

Lord God, your ways are greater than ours. We cannot discern your purposes yet you call us to do your will. Give to the leaders of our nation a firm commitment to the standards of your kingdom and determination to reject the evils of homelessness, poverty and exploitation . . .
Holy Lord, hear our cry,
And make us more like you.

Lord God, your love is deeper than ours. We cannot fathom its height or depth or length, yet you reveal it to us in your Son Jesus Christ. Give to those who are in need a sense of your loving presence, an awareness of your Holy Spirit comforting and sustaining them . . .
Holy Lord, hear our cry,
And make us more like you, as we grow in faith and increase in vision of your Son, Jesus Christ, Amen.

ALL-AGE ADDRESS

The majority of churchgoers have a rather flawed concept of God's call. Even in a day when lay involvement is emphasised, many still have the idea that God only calls clergy and mission workers. If they accept that they have been called, say, to serve on the PCC, the chances are they'll regard this as secondary, or of lower standing in God's kingdom. It's therefore vital to make clear that whatever God calls each individual to do for him, he counts all contributions as of equal value. Every Christian is called by God. Isaiah's call was dramatic but its

pattern is repeated throughout the history of God's dealings with his people. There are three stages. Isaiah is prepared for his prophetic ministry, he is commissioned for it, and he's equipped to fulfil it.

For the first stage find a youngster who regularly practises sport or dancing. Get them to demonstrate how they prepare for a match or performance. God doesn't necessarily want us to keep fit like that, but he always prepares us for the task he gives us. Isaiah's ministry was to the Temple and the senior figures of government. He had to take them God's message, so he was already in those circles before his call. Everything that happens in our lives, good or bad, happy or sad, is part of God's preparing of us for his ministry.

At the right time he brings us to stage two – the commissioning. Invite a Scout or Guide to come up, and ask them about how they officially became members of that movement. A Scout or Guide doesn't just become a member. He or she has to be recognised by the organisation as one. God may not ask us to take part in a formal ceremony, but he makes it quite clear that we have his authority. Whatever we do for Christ we do in his name, on his authority. The Church has always known this, and there are special services which underline her acknowledgement of certain ministries, such as ordination.

Stage three is the equipping. Ask someone to bake a cake, but don't mention any ingredients. When the lack of resources is pointed out, explain that your instruction depends on the right equipment. This you can then produce. In the same way, God doesn't expect us to go it alone. He's promised us all we need to minister in his name. When Isaiah was commissioned by God in that remarkable vision, God gave him just the words for the situation he was in. He knew what he was saying and doing was not something he'd invented. He had the authority of the King of kings and had been equipped by him, too! If we do things in our own strength we'll soon feel like giving up. When we let God speak to us and resource us, we can be sure that what we do isn't in vain.

Jeremiah – God's Promise

On the whole Jeremiah wasn't a happy man. That's hardly surprising considering his circumstances. Death threats were made against him, he was thrown into a very nasty pit, he managed to alienate himself from the whole court and government, and few people listened to him. On several occasions he vented his anger and frustration at God. The book which contains his prophecies doesn't appear at first sight to offer a great deal to the average all-age service. Somehow, doom and gloom on this scale don't quite fit the bill. But there is a message of hope for the future.

Unlike Isaiah, who moved in the highest circles, Jeremiah was of humbler background. He had little self-confidence, and was temperamentally best suited to a quiet life. Yet his ministry lasted over many years, right through Josiah's reign and into the exile. He appears to have come from a priestly family, but some of his harshest words are directed at the priesthood. Scholars have a variety of opinions about dating some passages, but whenever they were first uttered, few of Jeremiah's oracles could be described as optimistic. The one hopeful section comes in the 'Book of Consolation' (chapters 30–33), and here there's scope for a service theme. Not only is there an overarching sense of God's promise, but in the picture of Jeremiah buying a field we have also a tangible demonstration that God intends to keep his word.

Probably the best option is to link the promises with the warnings. Both are part of Jeremiah's ministry and are equally relevant to our own Christian lives now. We can no more ignore God's warnings than could Jeremiah's hearers

– if we don't obey God's instructions there are inevitable consequences. But if we follow his ways, however falteringly at times, we'll be in no doubt that God always keeps his promises.

READINGS

Jeremiah 1:4–10/2:4–8/5:11–19/7:1–11/8:4–12/18:1–10/23:1–8/30:8–11/31:2–6/7–14/31–34/32:1–15/36–44/33:14–22/Psalm 25/42/43/130/Romans 4:13–25/Galatians 3:26–4:7/Hebrews 10:32–39/Matthew 12:9–21/13:24–30/Mark 11:12–19/John 16:17–24

HYMNS

Traditional
All my hope on God is founded
Praise the Lord! Ye heavens adore him
My hope is built on nothing less
In heavenly love abiding
O God, our help in ages past

Modern
Rejoice, rejoice
If my people
Our confidence is in the Lord
Great is the lord and most worthy
We'll walk the land

CONFESSION

Almighty God, your promises are for everyone. You turn away no-one who comes to you in penitence and faith. We are sorry for the times when we have ignored your gracious call. Forgive us for not turning back to you. Have mercy upon us, save us from our sins, and bring us the joy of your salvation through the death and resurrection of our Saviour Jesus Christ, Amen.

God our loving Father have mercy upon you, forgive you all your sins, pardon you for all your wrongdoing and bring you the joy of his eternal salvation through Jesus Christ our Lord, Amen.

INTERCESSION

In obedience to the voice of our Heavenly Father, we turn to him in faith with our prayers, saying:
Merciful Lord, hear our prayer,
And let our cry come to you.

You have called the Church to bring your message of judgement and mercy to a hostile world. May all who acknowledge you as Lord declare your word without fear or caution, yet remain sensitive to those who listen. In particular we pray . . .
Merciful Lord, hear our prayer,
And let our cry come to you.

You have called those who govern us to follow the ways of justice and peace. May all in authority look to you as the one who gives them authority, and leads us in the right paths. In particular we pray . . .
Merciful Lord, hear our prayer,
And let our cry come to you.

You have called us to show your compassion and care to the suffering and needy. May they experience the touch of your healing hand outstretched to them in their time of pain. In particular we pray . . .
Merciful Lord, hear our prayer,
And let our cry come to you.

You call us now to remain faithful to your calling, to speak boldly for you and to serve you without counting the cost. May we know your strength within, to face the conflict without.
Merciful Lord, hear our prayer,
And let our cry come to you. Receive

our requests and answer them according to your gracious will for the sake of your Son, our Saviour Jesus Christ, Amen.

ALL-AGE ADDRESS

The theme of this talk is promises, so start by explaining that we all make promises – and often break them, too. We can promise to do something, and then forget about it. We can promise to do better, but then slip up again. God never breaks his promises. He made promises to his people. If they followed him and obeyed his law they would know his guidance and protection. But if they tried to go their own way, not keeping to his commandments and staying true to him, they would suffer the consequences.

1) Some promises have a condition attached. Offer someone a sweet (or other small reward!) and say they can have it – provided they fulfil some condition first, such as fetching something or fulfilling a simple task. Make sure you keep your promise! Promises aren't always in the nature of a reward, though. We might promise someone punishment if they fail to co-operate or behave pleasantly. But in either case the fulfilment of the promise depends on something else happening first.

2) Other promises have no conditions. Offer someone else a sweet, saying all they need to do is come up and take it. The only 'condition' is that the recipient believes the promise and acts on it. Explain that when God promises us forgiveness and freedom he doesn't add any conditions. All we need to do is receive what he's promised to give.

Illustrate this from Jeremiah's ministry, pointing out that it was Israel's refusal to believe God or act on his word that landed them in such a mess.

3) Finally, give someone a Smartie and promise them the whole packet later on as a thank you for helping. The one sweet is a token of the promise yet to be fulfilled. God was saying to his people that whatever happened he would never break the promise he'd made. They would suffer for being rebellious, but eventually God would act to release them and restore them to himself. Jeremiah's hearers took no notice and refused to accept this. Nevertheless God did keep to his word and in Jesus we see all his promises fulfilled.

Hosea – God's Love

Hosea is probably the best known of the minor prophets (minor in length rather than significance!). He was the earliest of the writing prophets, some time before the northern kingdom was overrun and dispersed by the Assyrians. In some ways he has much in common with Jeremiah, but the whole book as we have it is permeated by God's deep and indestructible love for his people. It's not easy to handle the question of Hosea's marriage in an all-age service, but it's so basic to the message, that whether we see it as a picture or a real event, it has to be taken into account. We know very little about Hosea, and such evidence as we have tells us only what he said. We can't even be sure how his words were received, though history suggests they were at best ignored.

His own life was an illustration of what he had to preach. Hosea's marriage to Gomer was a total disaster and the names of their children symbolise this. Likewise God had a disastrous relationship with his people. They'd treated him as an unfaithful wife treats her husband, spurning his love and dismissing the pain they were causing. The worship of the living God, Yahweh, had become mixed up with all kinds of other worship offered to foreign idols. Abominable heathen practices had become absorbed into Israel's religion. They had to recognise how seriously they had broken the Covenant with God, and what were the implications of this. Yet Hosea also had to convey God's incredible love, his determination to bring them back from the way of destruction.

*We are called to proclaim God's love above all else, but that doesn't mean we can ignore evil. Love is demanding, and cannot exist where those demands aren't met. God's love never changes or dimi-*nishes, but we can't experience it if we turn our back on him and look elsewhere. A relationship has to have two-way traffic. Hosea reveals to us more than any other Old Testament book the extent of our Father's love and the lengths he'll go to in order to bring us back to him, and he calls for a response.*

READINGS
Hosea 1:2–11/3:1–5/6:1–6/10:1–8/11:1–11/14:1–9/Psalm 13/31:1–8/36/57/86:1–10/103/136/Romans 5:1–11/Ephesians 2:1–10/1 John 3:1–10/Luke 15:11–32/John 14:15–27/17:20–26

HYMNS
Traditional
Love divine, all loves excelling
God is love: let Heaven adore him
O the deep, deep love of Jesus
My song is love unknown
O love of God

Modern
Such love
Thank you for the Cross
You laid aside your majesty
O let the Son of God enfold you
My Lord, what love is this

CONFESSION
Come let us return to the Lord and say:
**Lord our God,
in our sin we have avoided your call.
Our love for you is like the mist,
disappearing in the heat of the sun.
Have mercy on us.
Bind up our wounds and bring us
back to the foot of the cross, through
Jesus Christ our Lord, Amen.**

May the God of love bring you back to himself, forgive you your sins, and assure you of his eternal love in Jesus Christ our Lord, Amen.

INTERCESSION
We come into the presence of God
who brings us back to himself, saying:
Lord of love,
Fill our hearts today.

Loving Father, you look on this world
in sadness as you see it full of evil and
bitterness, hatred and violence. Help
us to bring your all-embracing love
into areas of darkness and pain,
especially . . .
Lord of love,
Fill our hearts today.

Loving Father, you look on the Church
in sadness as you see it torn apart by
division and its witness weakened.
Help us to realise anew the extent of
your love and share it with those
around, especially . . .
Lord of love,
Fill our hearts today.

Loving Father, you look with sadness
on your suffering children, whose
lives are spoiled by illness, unemployment, poverty and fear. Help us to
show them your great love and compassion, especially . . .
Lord of love,
**Fill our hearts today with your love,
make us more like Jesus, and make us
strong to do your will by the power of
the Holy Spirit, Amen.**

ALL-AGE ADDRESS
The mass media have left in many
people an abiding image of love as
soft-focus romantic slush! Romance is
obviously a vital ingredient in the love
of husband and wife, but it's hardly
the whole story. Roses and chocolates
are lovely symbols, but a lot more is
needed for a deep, loving relationship.
Quite apart from any false expecta
tions it may arouse, this view of love
can cause misunderstandings about
the nature of God's love. If possible
invite a newly-married couple, or a
couple planning their wedding, to be
interviewed about their relationship.
You'll probably have to brief the couple about the kind of answers you're
after.

1) The first area to highlight through
your questions is that love makes us
feel special. Out of all the other people
he/she could have chosen, it's me!
When we fall in love we want to spend
our lives with that someone special,
similarly God wants us to enter into a
special relationship with him.

2) The next point to make is that real
love is durable. It survives even when
things go badly wrong. It wouldn't be
much of a relationship if when the
husband caught a cold and the wife
said she didn't love him when his nose
was runny! Try to get the couple to
explain how they love each other
whatever the circumstances. God's
love for us doesn't change, either.

3) The third point is that love is about
giving (contrast this with the 'getting'
mentality of the world around). Most
partners give up something for each
other. God gave up his own Son
because he loved us so much.

4) Finally persuade the couple to express how their love for each other has
grown. We grow in our love for God as
we know his love in our hearts.

Although it's nothing like as effective as asking a real couple questions,
you could instead use four drawings
on the overhead projector (OHP) or
flip-chart to make the same points. A
good artist will depict how true love
makes us feel special, lasts forever, is
willing to sacrifice self interest, and
grows deeper. As you make these
points, use verses from Hosea to
underline their truth.

Amos – God's Justice

Of all the Old Testament prophets Amos now seems the most contemporary. In a society plagued by injustice, oppression, exploitation and selfishness, his voice seems as powerful and his message as relevant as when he first spoke. The herdsman from Tekoa wasn't too well received by his contemporaries, however – Amaziah felt Amos would be much better occupied looking after his animals. After all, what does a shepherd know about religion?

Amos' message packs a powerful punch. It hammers at the way in which even the church has become engulfed by the tide of materialism and self-centredness. It exposes the shallowness of much of our workshop. Most of all it highlights our frequent failure to endorse or stand up for the standards of justice and compassion which are fundamental to God's character. Amos was disliked because he challenged the very basis of most religious practice and attitudes.

Amos' message was delivered to a very wealthy society. Under the long reign of Jeroboam II Israel had become prosperous, standing on several trade routes. The picture of affluence in Amos is typical of that period. Nowhere does Amos condemn wealth. He attacks those who've become wealthy by exploiting the poor, perverting justice and trading dishonestly. Nor does he dismiss religious ritual per se. Rather, he writes off worship which is concerned only with external form and forgets that righteousness has to be the starting point. Hypocrisy is a particularly insidious sin. All of us are prone to it. We enter church without a thought for the less well-off, the marginalised or the downtrodden. Our material comforts occupy far more of our time than caring for others. To convey this is to issue a challenge. At the end of the day, words are meaningless if they're not accompanied by action.

READINGS
Amos 3:1–10/5:4–15/18–27/8:1–10/9:11–15/Psalm 9:1–12/36/72:1–14/97/Colossians 3:12–17/James 5:1–6/1 John 3:11–20/Matthew 25:31–46/Luke 12:13–21/18:18–30

HYMNS
Traditional
Help us to help each other, Lord
Lord Christ, who on thy heart
God of grace and God of glory
Glorious things of thee are spoken
Lord, speak to me

Modern
When I needed a neighbour
Make me a channel of your peace
Restore, O Lord
Who can sound the depths of sorrow
O Lord, the clouds are gathering

CONFESSION
Almighty God, ruler of Heaven and earth, we have failed to live up to your standards. We have disregarded the cry of the poor, and left the needy without hope. Our worship has been more concerned with appearance than obedience. Forgive our hypocrisy and lack of care and have mercy upon us. Fill our hearts with compassion and a commitment to demonstrate your love, as revealed to us in Jesus Christ our Lord, Amen.

Almighty God, whose arms of mercy are always open to those who confess their sins, have mercy upon you, cleanse you from all that is wrong, and restore you to himself for the sake of his Son, our Saviour Jesus Christ, Amen.

INTERCESSION

God of glory we pray for your justice
to rule this world as we say:
Merciful Lord, your Kingdom come,
Your will be done.

We pray for a world full of injustice
and oppression; for those whose lives
are scarred by ill-treatment and fear;
for those who struggle to overcome
evil with good. We bring before you
. . . Guide the leaders of the world and
all with power, that they may use it
rightly, and for the good of all.
Merciful Lord, your kingdom come,
Your will be done.

We pray for the church in places of
tension and wickedness; for those who
serve you in the face of threats; for
Christians whose faith is tested by the
surrounding hatred and insecurity.
We bring before you . . . Guide your
people, that they may boldly proclaim
your truth and spread your good
news.
Merciful Lord, your kingdom come,
Your will be done.

We pray for those known to us who
are in difficult situations; for any
without jobs or livelihood; for any
without home or friends; for any
without health and strength, or
lacking in joy. We bring before you . . .
Comfort and heal them, that they may
know your peace within.
Merciful Lord, your Kingdom come,
**Your will be done. Work in us and
through us, give us the mind of Christ
to bring consolation and hope, and
help us to worship you in spirit and in
truth, through Christ our Lord, Amen.**

ALL-AGE ADDRESS

It's unfortunate that some years ago
there appeared to be a dichotomy
between those who believed in the
'pure gospel' and those more concerned with social issues. More recently this has surfaced in some of the
arguments about whether or not the
Church should become involved in
political issues. There's no question of
choosing one or the other, however. A
wholehearted commitment to the gospel of Christ has to embrace a proper
concern for the underprivileged, expressed not just in occasional charity,
but in political action as well.

Amos mentions four particular
areas of wrongdoing in his prophetic
oracles – hypocritical religious cere-
monies; oppression of the poor and
weak; false dealings; and perverted
justice. Such a direct approach as
Amos takes is best treated directly. To
illustrate each point you'll need a few
prepared 'actors'. For example, shady
business dealings could involve one
shopkeeper and an obviously poor
customer (eg tatty clothes, little cash).
The shopkeeper could blatantly over-
charge either by use of impromptu
dialogue or by a commentary on the
situation. Amos' mention of scales
suggests a good prop! This would lead
on to how the poor are oppressed.
One possibility here is to have someone dressed in rags working hard at a
menial task, while another lounges in
a luxurious chair with a bottle of
champagne – either dialogue or commentary would clarify that the former
is paying for the latter's enjoyment. A
courtroom scene could come next,
with a magistrate or judge behaving in
a suitably corrupt way, letting off a
wealthy wrongdoer but punishing
harshly someone poor. For the final

scene, gather the 'wealthy' characters into a pew and encourage them to be pious and ostentatiously holy. Postures for prayer, hearty singing and devout talk will all make the point that hypocrisy in worship is not acceptable to God. It's no use pretending to be religious and good in church if our everyday lives don't reflect what we claim to believe. Everything we do in the way of worship is only acceptable to God if we share his love and compassion for the poor and needy, and keep to the standards of his kingdom, by being honest, fair and just.

Responding to Jesus

There are many ways of using the vast variety of material in the Gospels. There's a great deal to be said for following an idea through them. In this Decade of Evangelism it's worth taking a special look at how different people responded to Jesus coming into their lives in one way or another. I've tried to use some less obvious examples and include a variety of situations. Not all responded positively, and that is a particularly important issue if there are some at the service who wouldn't normally attend worship, or who are less than sympathetic to the Christian faith. Underlying all five examples is the challenge to each of us, whatever stage we may have reached in our pilgrimage, to hear what the Lord is saying to us and to respond to him in love and faith.

Responding to a Star

Unlike the other examples in this section, the Magi did not initially respond to Jesus as a person. All they knew of him was that he was to be the King of the Jews, so they brought him gifts to symbolise his kingship. We know little about these people, despite their frequent appearances in Nativity plays and on Christmas cards. It seems probable they were Eastern astrologers, who'd seen a remarkable star and looked it up in their charts and tables. How typical of God! The most important event in human history bypasses completely the government, the monarchy, the religious top brass and the civil service. Instead, the first people to receive the news of God intervening in the affairs of mankind by sending his Son to become one of us are a few scruffy shepherds out in the fields and some pagan intellectuals! Yet their response is acceptable to God, and quite unlike Herod's, or the Scribes' and Pharisees' reaction. More important even than the gifts is their worship of the new-born king.

Clearly this account of a response to Jesus is most suitable at Christmas or the Epiphany. It highlights the implications of the birth of Christ. For many the temptation will be to put him away until next year, to fail to recognise the significance of that baby boy. The long journey of these wise men (probably lasting weeks if not months) just to worship Jesus, of whom they knew so little, points us to the Cross, where Jesus gave his life thirty three years later for the salvation of all mankind. We know far more than they could have done about Jesus' real identity and purpose. How can we offer him less than the worship of our hearts and lives?

READINGS
Isaiah 60:1–3/Jeremiah 23:1–8/Micah 5:2–5a/Psalm 29/68:24–35/136:1–15/ Romans 12:1–8/2 Corinthians 8:8–15/ Revelation 4/Matthew 2:1–12/Mark 12:41–44/Luke 7:36–50

HYMNS
Traditional
As with gladness men of old
We three kings of Orient are
O worship the Lord in the beauty
Brightest and best
In the bleak midwinter

Modern
At this time of giving
I want to worship the Lord
Father in Heaven, how we love you
Let our praise be to you
I give you all the honour

CONFESSION
King of kings, we come into your presence recognising our utter unworthiness to stand before you. We have often failed to acknowledge you as Lord of our lives.
Father forgive us,
And cleanse us from our sins.

We have often failed to live up to the standards of your Kingdom or obey your commands.
Father forgive us,
And cleanse us from our sins.

We have often failed to put the interests and well-being of others above our own.
Father, forgive us,
And cleanse us from our sins.

We have often failed to give to you even a small part of what you have given us.
Father, forgive us,
And cleanse us from our sins.

We have often failed to worship you in spirit and in truth.
Father, forgive us,
And cleanse us from our sins. Help us to see you more clearly and to offer you all that we have and are for the sake of your Son Jesus Christ, Amen.

INTERCESSION
Lord Jesus, King of kings yet born in a stable, we worship you and offer our praises to your holy name. As the wise men were guided to you by the brightness of a star, so may we be led into your presence. May we offer you the gift of our lives and serve you joyfully for the sake of Jesus Christ our Lord, Amen.

Heavenly Father, you sent your Son into this world to be the Prince of Peace. We ask you to bring your peace to places which only know conflict and hatred . . . We ask you to make us channels of your peace in our homes, our schools, our places of work and our local community . . . We ask you to fill with your peace anyone known to us who is suffering or in need . . . As we offer you ourselves in worship, fill us with your peace and send us out to serve you with joy, through Christ our Lord, Amen.

ALL-AGE ADDRESS
The visit of the wise men clearly suggests the theme of our gifts to God. An address could well be fitted around a traditional Epiphany procession. This may not happen in your church, so an alternative is to concentrate on the gifts we can offer God, drawing parallels with the wise men and their offerings.
1) Gold speaks of great value, so display first an object of value (a piece of jewellery, perhaps, or small antique). Emphasise that God isn't interested in our possessions as such, but in our attitude to them. At this point produce a cheque book. Explain that God gives us everything we have and that we can only give back to him what he's already given us. We offer our money, because it sums us up – our work, our homes, our priorities. If we value our relationship with God, it'll be no hardship to offer him our money and the things we treasure.
2) Frankincense speaks of holiness, so here a diary can be brought out. God wants all of our lives to be holy, not just on Sunday but every day. He doesn't want our homes to be full of incense (or even necessarily our churches!), but it's certainly his will that they should be filled with his love and truth. Holiness isn't about trying to be perfect or pious. We become more holy as we allow God to enter our lives day by day.
3) Myrrh speaks of Jesus' death. He died for our forgiveness and to set us free from the power of sin and death. But we must be willing to confess our sins and be open to his forgiveness. Distribute at this point a small piece of paper to each person (it might be preferable with a larger congregation to do this earlier as people arrive), and ensure that spare pencils are available. Get each person to write down a sin for which they seek God's forgiveness and then fold the paper up. Collect them up and dispose of them, if possible by burning in a fireproof container. This is a very strong picture and needs careful handling. It should be emphasised that when God forgives us, he treats our sins as though they'd never happened. This address is particularly good when followed by the Eucharist, at which our money is brought up to the altar, and we then kneel to offer ourselves in penitence and faith.

Responding to a Call

Andrew has the distinction of being one of the first of Jesus' disciples to follow him. Unlike his more upfront brother Simon Peter, Andrew doesn't appear quite so often in the Gospel narratives – he didn't become one of the 'inner circle' around Jesus. Yet he will always be remembered as the disciple who went to find his brother and bring him to the Lord. He recognised straightaway who Jesus was and didn't hesitate either to follow him or to fetch his brother.

St Andrew's Day is a reminder of God's call to us to proclaim the good news to those around us, so evangelism is the theme of this section. It's a pity that evangelism is so frequently associated with large scale crusades and high profile speakers. That's not to sneer at evangelists like Billy Graham (where would church numbers be today without his ministry?), but to underline the importance of one-to-one relationships. A recent survey revealed that the most fruitful form of evangelism in the church today is husbands or wives sharing the good news with their unbelieving partners! In fact, all the evidence from major evangelistic missions is that their 'success' is largely dependent on Christians who have prayed for and brought along their non-Christian friends.

In a world so full of bad news, it's vital to stress that the Gospel is good news. it won't solve all the world's problems overnight, but it's the best possible news for all who respond to the voice of Jesus.

READINGS
Genesis 45:16–28/2 Kings 7:3–11/
Isaiah 40:9–11/Psalm 40:1–10/98/Acts
13:32–40/1 Corinthians 15:1–11/
Colossians 1:24–2:5/Luke 4:14–22/
15:1–7/John1:35–42

HYMNS
Traditional
We have a gospel to proclaim
Go forth and tell
Tell out my soul
O breath of life
We have heard a joyful sound

Modern
One shall tell another
How lovely on the mountains
It only takes a spark
From the sun's rising
All earth was dark

CONFESSION
Loving Father, you call us to follow you and tell others of your saving love. We are sorry for not heeding your voice and are ashamed at our reluctance to make your love known. Forgive our deafness and slowness and deliver us from all our sins. Place in our hearts a spirit of obedience, we pray, that we may hear you speak and rejoice to do your will, for Christ's sake, Amen.

Almighty God, the merciful redeemer of all who kneel in repentance before him, have mercy upon you, pardon and deliver you from all sin, and grant you the joy of his kingdom, both now and in eternity, through Christ our Lord, Amen.

INTERCESSION
As we bring our prayers and requests to the Lord who calls us we say:
Lord Jesus, we hear your voice,
Help us to obey.

Lord Jesus, you call us to fulfil your great commission and preach the Gospel to all people. Help us to see where the fields are white and ready

to harvest . . .
Lord Jesus, we hear your voice,
Help us to obey.

Lord Jesus, you call us to be holy as
you are holy. Help us to see in our
own lives and in society where things
are not as they should be . . .
Lord Jesus, we hear your voice,
Help us to obey.

Lord Jesus, you call us to pray for our
world and government. Help us to
share your anger at the evil which
surrounds us . . .
Lord Jesus, we hear your voice,
Help us to obey.

Lord Jesus, you call us to care for those
in need or suffering. Help us to feel
your compassion for them and bring
them your comfort and love . . .
Lord Jesus, we hear your voice,
Help us to obey.

Lord Jesus, you call us to follow you
without counting the cost. Help us to
serve you willingly and with
resolution . . .
Lord Jesus, we hear your voice,
**Help us to obey, so that one day we
will hear you say 'Well done.' This we
ask through Jesus Christ our Lord,
Amen.**

ALL-AGE ADDRESS

This talk needs a bit of preparation.
During the previous week find and cut
out newspaper headlines which are
either good or bad. As an example,
peace in one part of the world could be
contrasted with war elsewhere, or
news of share price rises or economic
recovery might be offset by a redun-
dancy notice or the latest unemployment figures. In talking about these

news items, explain how good news
for one person might be bad news for
someone else. In this world good news
always has a limit. A victory for Spurs
means a defeat for Aston Villa, for
example.

The good news about Jesus is for
all time, all places and all people.

1) Although he lived at a particular
time, his death on the Cross and
resurrection have brought new life to
everyone who believes and trusts in
him. They're just as effective now as
they were two thousand years ago to
enable us to be forgiven and set free.
An OHP slide or flip-chart picture of
Jesus and someone in twentieth century dress will help make this point.

2) Jesus also lived in a particular place,
but his salvation isn't just for the Jews
or those living in that part of the
Middle East. It doesn't matter what
cultural background you come from,
what colour skin you have, or what
language you speak. Jesus' saving love
embraces the whole world. A picture
of people from different parts of the
world will underline this.

3) Jesus also died for all people – no-
one is too bad for him to save. Everyone who receives his love in their
hearts becomes his child, part of God's
family. A picture of a crowd will
illustrate this. Point out that human
beings make unfair distinctions between each other, but God never does.
His good news isn't limited or tempor-
ary. It's the only good news that's
guaranteed to last for ever!

Responding to Jesus' Presence

Martha and Mary have been the subject of many sermons on the importance of not overworking. However, it seems unlikely that they were included by Luke as a warning against hyperactivity! There's no need to create a false division between work and rest. That was Martha's mistake. She wasn't doing wrong by working around the house, but she needed to learn that Mary sitting at Jesus' feet, enjoying his company and teaching, was just as valid. In effect she criticised her sister for laziness, because she hadn't thought beyond her immediate tasks. We aren't really told whether Martha was cleaning around especially for Jesus' arrival, or whether she thought the place looked a tip. She may not have been trying to impress the Lord.

However, the point of the story is that these two sisters responded differently to Jesus' arrival. One response was appropriate, the other wasn't. Martha failed to understand that whatever the house may have looked like, it was more important to listen to Jesus and enjoy his presence. We tend to react like Martha, especially when as Christians we get together. A sudden corporate urge to go into overdrive seems to beset many churches, and while they may work themselves into a lather doing many good things, they miss out on spending time quietly with God, listening to him speaking, and seeking his will. Many of the activities are perfectly good and worthy, but if they replace times of meditation and refreshment they'll soon become a chore. By spending time with God in prayer, we'll discover what he wants us to do and receive strength for doing it.

READINGS
Genesis 1:26–2:3/Exodus 20:8–11/Isaiah 30:15–18/Psalm 62/91/Romans 5:1–5/Ephesians 2:14–22/Philippians 4:4–9/Matthew 6:25–34/11:25–30/Luke 10:38–42

HYMNS
Traditional
Dear Lord and Father of Mankind
Jesus, the very thought of thee
When all your mercies
Make me a captive, Lord
I need thee every hour

Modern
As the deer pants for the water
When I feel the touch
In moments like these
Be still, for the presence of the Lord
Let me have my way among you

CONFESSION
Heavenly Father, we look at our lives and see how little time we spend with you. We are always busy, our minds distracted by the pressures of life. Our hearts are never still and our souls never at rest. Forgive our foolishness and sin, and show us your mercy. Bring us back to Jesus' feet and open our ears to his loving voice, in whose name we pray, Amen.

Almighty God, the all-merciful Father, grant you pardon and deliverance from all your sins, time for repentance and amendment of life and the peace of his Holy Spirit through Jesus Christ our Lord, Amen.

INTERCESSION
We bring our prayers to the Prince of Peace, saying:
Lord of Eternity,
Grant us your peace.

Your peace is needed in so many places around the world. We ask for it especially in . . . Bless those who labour to bring peace where there is conflict and still the hearts of those who seek violence.
Lord of Eternity,
Grant us your peace.

Your serenity is needed by your people throughout the world. We ask it especially for the church in . . . Bless those who bear witness to the reconciling love of Jesus and make them channels of your peace.
Lord of Eternity,
Grant us your peace.

Your rest is needed by some who are known to us. We ask it especially for . . . Bless and comfort those who suffer from ill-health, depression or anxiety, and help them find in you the source of all peace.
Lord of Eternity,
Grant us your peace. As we work and serve you, help our restless hearts to find their rest only in you, through the merits of Jesus our Saviour, Amen.

ALL-AGE ADDRESS
The inevitable bustle and noise of an all-age service may seem to militate against the message of this small domestic scene from Luke's Gospel. It may even feel perverse! However, there aren't many of us who don't need to learn more of responding appropriately to the presence of Jesus. Whether as individuals struggling with our various priorities, or as church fellowships striving to work out a reasonable pattern of activities, we all suffer from the tendency to try and prove ourselves, either to God or each other. As Martha discovered,

we've got nothing to prove to Jesus! This talk is aimed at demonstrating the need for balance in our lives. If we overdo one element against another, everything goes haywire.

You'll need a pair of scales for this illustration, ideally the old-fashioned kind with weights. Take some stones of various sizes and label them with an indelible marker pen. Some should be words associated with our work, and others with our leisure time. 'Overtime', 'Staying late', 'Business trips' etc, could be balanced against 'sport', 'family' and 'entertainment'. The exact words used will need adaptation to local circumstances. It's fairly easy to demonstrate what happens when, for example, work becomes too 'heavy'. Then move on to church activities, which you can compare with 'prayer', 'meditation' or 'fasting'. All these things are legitimate. Evangelism is a vital part of every church's life, and the PCC can't be shelved indefinitely! But if the whole congregation is rushing about doing many good works, no-one will have time to stop and find out if these were the good works God had in mind.

God wants us to work – it's part of his created order. But he also wants us to rest and enjoy the world, as he did. He wants us to do his will and serve him, but not at the expense of praying and listening to him. We need to identify the right time for the latter, as Mary did. In the end she was the one who made the appropriate response to Jesus, and gained the benefit.

Responding to the Challenge

The three previous examples in this section are all people who in one way or another responded positively to Jesus. However, not everyone did. The rich young man who wanted to follow Jesus is a good illustration of why some people shy away from the unavoidable challenge he presents. It isn't clear what his motivation was in coming to Jesus, but it seems to have been genuine enough. No doubt, like others, he was attracted by this remarkable rabbi, whose teaching seemed so much more profound than anything given by other teachers. In the end this man's problems came down to wealth. He had no problems with God's law. He was very devout and had a sincere desire to please God. The trouble was, he had too much to lose. Jesus didn't particularly mind him owning a lot – it was just that his attitude to it would be a barrier to truly following Christ.

Unless you live in a very well-to-do area you won't have many in your congregation who are really wealthy, but there are many other obstacles which prevent or hinder a positive response to God's call. Materialism and ownership are almost a disease, even among the poor. The craving to possess things is apparently insatiable in every stratum of society. Cynicism is another serious handicap for many (well-fuelled by the media), along with its close cousin apathy. Nothing is taken really seriously; everything is fair game to be made fun of. Time pressure is a real problem for many, as is the availability of so many other activities. This rich young man, about whom we know so little, needles us into looking at our own response to the challenge of following Jesus. There is a cost to be taken into account.

READINGS
1 Kings 3:4–14/Ecclesiastes 5:8–20/
Isaiah 5:8–17/Psalm 49/128/
2 Corinthians 9:6–15/1 Timothy 6:6–
12/James 2:1–13/Matthew 19:16–29/
Luke 12:13–21/16:19–31

HYMNS
Traditional
Thou who wast rich beyond all
   splendour
All for Jesus
I do not know what lies ahead
Take my life and let it be
O Jesus, I have promised

Modern
The greatest thing in all my life
He has showed you, O man
I want to walk with Jesus Christ
Seek ye first the Kingdom of God
Abba Father, let me be

CONFESSION
Almighty God, we have not loved you with all our heart and mind. We have backed away from the challenge of following you, preferring instead the things of this world. Forgive our unwillingness and pardon our rejection of your love. Make us faithful disciples and by your Spirit strengthen and equip us to do your will, through Jesus Christ our Lord, Amen.

God our Father, who forgives all who acknowledge their sins to him, have mercy upon you, pardon and deliver you from all your sins, and give you grace to obey his call and follow him in faith through Christ our Lord, Amen.

INTERCESSION

Lord Jesus, we bring our prayers to you in confidence and faith, saying:
Gracious Lord, as we follow you,
Increase our faith.

Lord Jesus, your will is that all people should know and love you. We ask you to help us express and demonstrate your love for those you have created . . . Bless your Church as she witnesses to your saving power, and give boldness and courage to all your people.
Gracious Lord, as we follow you,
Increase our faith.

Lord Jesus, your will is that all mankind should live together in harmony, ruled by your law of love. We ask you to help us live as citizens of this world and members of your Kingdom . . . Bless your people as they serve you in their nations and communities, and give them strength to uphold your standards.
Gracious Lord, as we follow you,
Increase our faith.

Lord Jesus, your will is that suffering and pain should be healed. We ask you to help us bring your compassion and care to those who are ill, afraid, grieving or in distress . . . Bless all who work in caring for the sick and needy, and give us hearts of love to reach out to them.
Gracious Lord, as we follow you,
Increase our faith, and as we hear your call, give us grace to rise up and follow you, for the sake of our Saviour Jesus Christ, Amen.

ALL-AGE ADDRESS

The rich young man of this narrative reminds us that humankind has an almost infinite capacity to put obstacles in the way of doing God's will. This idea for an address highlights those barricades (especially some twentieth century specialities!). It can be delivered either with 'live' illustrations or with cartoons of them on the OHP or flip-chart.

1) The most obvious from this story is money (demonstrated with a cheque book or high denomination banknote). Point out that while God doesn't mind us having money, it soon gets a hold over us. Making money and keeping hold of it very easily become a preoccupation which takes up far more time than worship, prayer and Christian service. If we aren't careful it holds us in a vice-like grip and then prevents us from responding when God calls us. As Jesus said, "You can't serve God and money".

2) If there's time extend this into our possessions. These could be antiques of some sort, luxury items or, for the children's benefit, toys. We spend vast amounts of time, energy and money on what we own or would like to own. We pore over catalogues (produce one or two) for hours, but not over the Bible, and dream of what it would be like if only we had . . . It's not just the very rich who are prone to this. Wrong attitudes to possessions are as much of an obstacle for those who don't have much as for those who do.

3) Relationships can also prove to be a huge stumbling-block to following God. Boy–girl friendships are an obvious example, but so are families. If

you can persuade a family to come forward at this point it's a powerful picture, especially if three or more generations can be represented. Stress that God wants us to enjoy family life, friendships and love. Indeed, neglecting family and loved ones is something God views very seriously and counts as sin. However, we aren't to love them more than him.

4) Television and video is another classic example of technology elbowing God out. (Hold up a videotape to make the point.) Both are excellent for occasional relaxation, and very important for the elderly and those shut in at home. But again, they soon take over, and God at best gets squeezed in between programmes.

5) Sport and leisure activities frequently take people away from worshipping on Sunday (get someone to appear in sports kit at this point), and so, increasingly, does work.

6) Perhaps the most insidious obstacle in the twentieth century is the cynicism and apathy which so pervades our society and implies that believing anything or even taking it seriously is somehow beneath contempt. This negative outlook is growing apace, and many are ready to laugh and poke fun at anything rather than face up to its demands. This isn't easy to illustrate, but older children will understand what is being said. Finish by saying that we give in to these obstacles and block God out without even realising it, because they're so much part of us. There's nothing wrong with them (except cynicism) and God's will is that we should work, love, live in families and communities and enjoy all the good things he's given us in the world. We must ask the Holy Spirit to keep our priorities right and ensure that Jesus is always our first consideration.

Responding to a Crisis

The choice of Pilate may seem a bit odd in that he tried to make no response at all to Jesus. But for that reaon he's possibly the most important for the twentieth century, because he tried to sit on the fence – and found he couldn't. There are many in our western culture who imagine they can reserve judgement on who Jesus was and how they should respond to him. Unfortunately it isn't possible. As Jesus himself pointed out, "whoever isn't for me is against me." Pilate was faced with a crisis when he met Jesus. That doesn't mean here an emergency (though from his point of view it nearly became one!). Rather, it was a crisis in the original Greek sense of the word – he had to make a decision, and nothing could get him out of it. However much he squirmed, Pilate went down in history as the man who let Jesus go to his death, albeit against his better judgement.

Pilate also indicates how easy it is to be swayed by a crowd. Popular opinion can be a dangerous thing, as those who've courted it have at times discovered. Pilate wanted no hassle or trouble. He was much happier when he could back off and devolve responsibility to someone else. After all, he was in a small and irrelevant backwater of the Roman Empire, not the sort of place where much was expected to happen. No doubt he felt that the question of what to do with Jesus was a matter for the local religious authorities. But it wouldn't go away – they could only act if he authorised it, and he feared more trouble if he refused. In the end he gave in to the crowd, with some doubts still assailing his peace of mind. In a society where the pressure of public opinion and the media is so strong, many are swayed by what they see as the common view. The role of Pilate in the Passion narratives gives the opportunity to challenge that passivity and the inclination to hold back on making a response. God demands a response from all of us, like it or not.

READINGS
Numbers 22:13–35/1 Kings 3:1–15/ Isaiah 52:13–53:12/Psalm 75/96/98/ Acts 10:34–43/1 Corinthians 11:23–32/ James 4:7–12/Matthew 13:24–30/John 12:44–50/John 19:1–16

HYMNS
Traditional
O for a closer walk with God
O the bitter shame and sorrow
O sacred Head, once wounded
When I survey the wondrous Cross
It is a thing most wonderful

Modern
Lord of the Cross of Shame
I have decided to follow Jesus
Come, see the beauty of the Lord
You laid aside your majesty
From Heaven you came

CONFESSION
Almighty God, we have done what is wrong in your eyes. Our sins are ever before us and we are unworthy to stand in your presence. Pardon and deliver us from all that stains our life, grant us hearts full of repentance, and by your great mercy bring us to eternal life through Christ our Lord, Amen.

God, the Father of all mercies, receives your prayer of penitence, forgives all that makes you unworthy of him, and grants you on this earth peace and freedom from guilt and in the life to come eternal joy, through Jesus Christ our Lord, Amen.

INTERCESSION

Heavenly Father, you sent your Son to die for our forgiveness. We offer you our worship and adoration:
Lord of love, we cry to you,
Hear your children's prayer.

Heavenly Father, Jesus died that we might be one in love and fellowship, yet the Church is divided and split. We pray that we and all your people may come together in unity . . .
Lord of love, we cry to you,
Hear your children's prayer.

Heavenly Father, Jesus died that by his wounds we might be healed, yet there is so much suffering and pain around us. We pray that those who govern us may recognise that their authority comes from you alone . . .
Lord of love, we cry to you,
Hear your children's prayer.

Heavenly Father, Jesus died that one day suffering and death should be destroyed forever, yet while we live on this earth people are ill, sad, lonely and distressed. We pray that they may know your love surrounding and holding them in their time of need . . .
Lord of love, we cry to you,
Hear your children's prayer.

Heavenly Father, Jesus died that we might walk in freedom and faith, yet we are still held back by the things of this world. We pray that we may be released from the chains of sin and fear to serve you joyfully.
Lord of love, we cry to you,
Hear your children's prayer for the glory of Christ your Son, our Lord, Amen.

ALL-AGE ADDRESS

For this talk, which is most obviously useful at Easter but could play a part at some other time, you'll need some OHP acetates or flipchart sheets with various excuses written on them why people won't commit themselves to Jesus. Another option is to have large cards held up by two people. The vital thing is that the words are visible. Two things stand out about Pilate – he wouldn't make a decision, and he was easily influenced by the crowd. Both are true of many people today.

What do people say when they won't face up to the challenge of Jesus? "I've got too much else on my plate at the moment"; "it's nothing to do with me"; "maybe when I'm older I'll think about it more"; "I'm sure my friend gets a lot out of it, but . . ." "you're welcome to your own beliefs – and so am I!". Briefly point out the flaw in each excuse. None of us ever have enough time, yet we always find time for what we want to do. If that one doesn't work when the vicar drops by, then the second is brought out – but on what grounds can the Christian faith be more applicable to one person than another? Delaying tactics are often in evidence. There's always a better time in the future to make a decision – although the future becomes the past very quickly, especially as we get older.

Reasonableness comes next – it's OK if you like that sort of thing, but I just don't respond to it. Surely, if a friend finds it makes sense to him, the most sensible way through is to investigate his claims, not to shelve them? The final point is on one level irrefutable – we all have a right to hold and express personal opinions. However, it isn't an argument about the truth and relevance of the Christian faith. All it really says is "I don't want to listen".

We're not really independent thinkers, even if we'd like to think of ourselves that way. Our views and thoughts are coloured by so many other outside pressures. Just as Pilate was cowed by a noisy crowd, so we're swayed by the 'crowd' of the late twentieth century – ill-defined public opinion as articulated by the media. If someone starts to show a touch more independence of thought his peers soon tow him into line. Your cards for this part of the talk could read: "Didn't you see on the TV last week . . .?"; "seventy per cent of the population can't be wrong"; "a friend of mine who knows about this said to me . . ."; "I don't want to look weird or stand out"; "small minorities aren't my cup of tea".

Again, try to refute the sort of arguments that underlie these expressions. There's always an assumption that TV and the press are telling the truth and can be relied on to provide unbiased evidence; statements from unnamed "friends" (or even named ones!) fall at the same hurdle. And why accuse all Christians of being weird or a tiny minority? Nowhere are active, committed Christians asked to behave in abnormal ways. There's no way to sit on the fence about Jesus. Those who try to remain 'neutral' will end up being pulled along by the crowd.

Finish this talk with a clear opportunity to respond. As we're confronted with the reality of Jesus' death which choice will we make?

Changed by Jesus

There's clearly a certain amount of overlap between the last section and this. Some of those who responded to Jesus did so because he'd changed their lives. Others found that in responding to him a change took place. The emphasis in these five service outlines is on the radical nature of the change that took place in the lives of the individuals chosen. Many others could have been taken, but these seemed to speak in a particular way in the context of all-age worship.

In each case, the transformation goes far beyond any superficial adjustment. It's important to keep emphasising that when Jesus takes hold of our lives and makes them different he affects us at the very deepest levels. It's also a process, not an event – we're changed 'from one degree of glory to another'. Jesus goes on changing us, making us more like him.

A New Vision

Bartimaeus is well-known enough as a New Testament character. Jesus healed many of blindness, but Bartimaeus is perhaps the most familiar. Maybe he has a name, which helps us remember. In any event, his lifestyle changed dramatically in the course of a few minutes, when Jesus came his way. In an age when those with physical handicaps are not only cared for, but encouraged to live as normal a life as possible, we find it hard to comprehend how someone so defenceless could be left to scrape a living together begging by the roadside. It doesn't really occur to us that illness or infirmity, especially when caused congenitally, might be the result of sin. Jesus, on another occasion (in John 9) had to point out to his disciples that sin wasn't the sole cause of conditions such as blindness, nor was it to be regarded as a punishment from God. As a result, we fail to understand the full extent of the healing miracle Jesus performed. For Bartimaeus it wasn't just a question of being able to see for the first time, wonderful though it no doubt was to enjoy vision and colour. It meant that no longer was he dependent on others' charity, that he could work for his living like sighted people. It meant that people would no longer think of him as a sinner, or contaminated by his parents' sin. Perhaps more than anything else it dealt with his own sense of sin and not being worth much. He'd probably have felt acutely aware of this burden of guilt. In one brief encounter, Jesus deals with the lot!

The Church has rediscovered its God-given ministry of healing in recent years, but the emphasis is still too often put on physical healing alone, rather than on the complete healing, the wholeness, that is characteristic of Jesus' ministry. Although in anatomical terms it was Bartimaeus'
eyesight *that was restored, his new vision represents many other elements of a new life. From the point of meeting Jesus onwards his life would never be the same again.*

READINGS
2 Kings 4:1–7/20:1–11/Isaiah 61:1–4/
Psalm 28/107:10–16/Romans 12:1–8/
Colossians 2:20–3:11/Philemon/Mark
1:21–34/10:46–52/John 9:18–34

HYMNS
Traditional
Lord, I was blind, I could not see
My song is love unknown
At even, 'ere the sun was set
Amazing grace
Jesus, lover of my soul

Modern
Open our eyes, Lord
Open your eyes
Praise you, Lord, for the wonder
Make way! Make way!
Go tell it on the mountain

CONFESSION
Lord Jesus, you gave seeing eyes to the blind and restored them to wholeness. We confess that we have wilfully shut our eyes to your presence and been unwilling to receive your healing grace. Have mercy on us, Lord, have mercy. Forgive our blindness and stubbornness and bring us to new and eternal life through Jesus Christ our Lord, Amen.

Almighty God, who has mercy on all who cry out to him in repentance and faith, meet you in your need, pardon and deliver you from all your sins and bring you the joy of his new and unending life, for the sake of Jesus Christ our Lord, Amen.

INTERCESSION
We come before the Lord who hears us call:
Open our eyes, Lord,
We want to see Jesus.

Lord, we bring to you our church, and the church throughout the world. May we have a fresh vision of your love and healing power. We pray especially . . .
Open our eyes, Lord,
We want to see Jesus.

Lord, we bring to you our world, and the place where we live. May we see more clearly how we are to be salt and light for your kingdom. We pray especially . . .
Open our eyes, Lord,
We want to see Jesus.

Lord, we bring to you our families and friends, all whom we love, and all for whom we are concerned. May they see the Lord Jesus in us and be drawn closer to him. We pray especially . . .
Open our eyes, Lord,
We want to see Jesus.

Lord, we bring to you the sick, the elderly, the fearful and the sad. May they see you coming alongside to comfort and sustain in their time of need. We pray especially . . .
Open our eyes, Lord,
We want to see Jesus.

Lord, we come before you ourselves with empty hands, trusting in your unending love. May we see you at work in our lives each day, and in each other.
Open our eyes, Lord,
We want to see Jesus in all his glory and worship him as king forever, in whose name we ask these things, Amen.

ALL-AGE ADDRESS

Yet another talk which involves blindfolds! The aim is to draw the parallels between the condition of blindness and our spiritual blindness. The first action is to blindfold one or two children. Explain that they've got a problem – you want them to fetch something from the other end of church and they've got to bring it to you. If you have a sound system, your mobility will be limited unless you have a radio microphone, so you may also need a 'guide'.

1) The first point to make is that a blind person has little idea of exactly where he is. Without help he'll wander round in circles, very disorientated. Add that many people in our society are like that – they can see well enough but their lives have little sense of purpose or direction.

2) The second point is that a blind person is particularly vulnerable to accidents and bumps, as your volunteers may well demonstrate! They aren't aware of the obstacles or barriers until too late. Those who live without Jesus find it much harder to cope with the difficulties of life, because they can't 'see' properly.

3) The third point is that they miss out on so much of life – colour, form, beauty etc. So do people who don't know Jesus for themselves. They have a whole dimension of their lives missing, though they may not realise it.

4) Point out finally that your two volunteers can't fulfil their task without help. You could persuade someone to guide them to their destination, but ideally they need their blindfolds removing. Then they can fetch the item themselves. That's what Jesus does for us. He doesn't just guide us; he actually takes off the things that stop us seeing. It's a whole new life, a life of freedom, like Bartimaeus was able to enjoy.

A New Mind

This healing miracle of Jesus deals with a problem which wasn't physical, at least in its origins. The illness in this case was mental and presumably spiritual, since it manifested itself in the context of the worship of God. Scholars may debate the exact nature of the man's condition, but whether he was mentally ill or demonically oppressed the effect of his encounter with Jesus was the same. It isn't exactly clear what triggered the outburst, but the presence of Jesus was not something he could handle.

We're not told much about this man, but it seems unlikely that he was able to engage in normal relationships with other people. The extent to which this was obvious on the outside may have affected others' view of him, but Jesus saw beneath the surface to his real needs. He knew the man's problems and went straight to the heart of them. As a result of meeting with Jesus he was made whole, set free, and able to live acceptably with other people. It was a dramatic change, one that couldn't but be noticed by everyone who knew him. No doubt their reactions were rather mixed. Whatever power could achieve such a miracle?

Jesus' authority is absolute – no situation is so desperate that he can't deal with it. It isn't a magic power, nor yet anything to do with New Age mysticism. The power of Jesus to confront and banish evil comes from his heavenly Father – no forces of evil can possibly stand against it. In a society which often fosters and commends the wrong kind of power, this life-changing encounter with Jesus reminds us of the source of all power and authority.

READINGS
Exodus 14:15–31/2 Kings 6:15–23/
Isaiah 40:25–31/Psalm 66/106:1–12/
114/Romans 15:14–22/Ephesians 1:15–23/Revelation 5/Mark 1:21–28/Luke 4:31–37/20:1–8

HYMNS
Traditional
All hail the power of Jesus' name
How sweet the name of Jesus sounds
Jesus the name high over all
May the mind of Christ my Saviour
Immortal love, for ever full

Modern
For this purpose
In the name of Jesus
There is power in the name of Jesus
All hail the Lamb
Yes, power belongs to you

CONFESSION
Lord Jesus, your power is greater than all the forces of evil. We are sorry for the times when we have trusted in our own strength.
Forgive us, Lord, for our lack of faith,
And show us your mercy.

We are sorry for the times when we have doubted your power to save and heal.
Forgive us, Lord, for our unbelief,
And show us your mercy.

We are sorry for the times when we have gone our own way and not thought about you.
Forgive us, Lord, for our waywardness,
And show us your mercy.

We are sorry for the times when we have justified our wrongdoing and forgotten your laws.
Forgive us, Lord, for our disobedience,
And show us your mercy for the sake of your Son, our Saviour Jesus Christ, Amen.

Almighty God, have mercy upon you and by his great power deliver you from the forces of evil for his name's sake, Amen.

INTERCESSION

Father God, all authority in Heaven and on earth belongs to you. Your power has defeated every other power at work in this world. We ask you to fill your people with the power of the risen Lord, that they may walk with you in victory. Grant to the Church courage to minister in the mighty name of Jesus, to counter and drive out all that is wicked, and to bring healing and wholeness to ravaged and hurting lives. May we trust your mighty arm to bring in your Kingdom of Light, through Jesus Christ our Lord, Amen.

Father in Heaven, bless and guide all in authority, especially our own government. May they stand up for righteousness and condemn evil, wherever it is seen in our society. As all authority is given by you, may they rule over us in accordance with your laws and govern us with your compassion, in Jesus' name, Amen.

Loving Father, we pray for all who are suffering through the forces of darkness – the homeless, the unemployed, the exploited, the rejected. In particular we name . . . May they feel your love surrounding them, and know your power at work in their lives, through Jesus Christ our Lord, Amen.

ALL-AGE ADDRESS

An all-age address is hardly the time or place for a lengthy psychological analysis, nor would anything more than a brief warning about the Occult and associated practises be in order. This talk requires a computerised hand-held 'personal organiser' and if available a personal computer which can produce graphics. It's best to avoid computer games as they'll be a major distraction, especially for the younger ones

Start by demonstrating what a small computer can do – calculate, store information and recall it, and so on. Then demonstrate that it's possible to use a computer creatively, by designing something simple and printing it out. If you don't own and can't operate one of these packages, ask the owner to do so for you. It may be necessary to do some preparation beforehand to avoid taking too much time. If no such technology is to hand within the congregation, try to obtain some examples of computer graphics which have been printed out. Emphasise how powerful the computer must be to make such calculations or designs possible. Having done this, say that each of us owns a computer infinitely more powerful than anything available in the shops. Our brain is the most amazing computer ever seen. Even a straightforward set of actions like those involved in driving a car would be beyond the capacity of a computer. Psychologists know that there are two sides to our brains, right and left, one handling all the rational thought processes and assimilating information, the other dealing with the creative functions.

God has given us our minds, and we can use them for good or evil purposes (compare a figure of evil such as Hitler with, for example, Mother Teresa). They can not only understand and store information about God's world, but can even share in his creative work. Most of all, our minds are able to handle relationships, unlike any piece of technology, however cleverly made. God has given us minds which experience feeling and emotion.

Finish the talk by explaining how Jesus healed the demoniac's mind and spirit. He brought wholeness to his thought processes, so that he could understand things properly and live in a normal relationship with other people. We may not suffer in quite the same way, but there are parts of all of us which need God's healing touch, areas of past hurt and unhappiness. Emphasise that Jesus' power to heal is so great that he can even sort out the parts that we find difficulty speaking about.

A New Lifestyle

The two previous examples of lives changed by Jesus were both in need of healing, in one case physical, in the other mental and spiritual. Zacchaeus wasn't ill at all. He was a rather sad little man, outwardly quite affluent and prosperous, but knowing in his heart of hearts that his gains were largely ill-gotten. From the little we are told about him, it seems probable that he had few friends and even less respect. For all his material success his life was pretty flat and empty. Tax-collectors aren't popular at the best of times, but when they work for an occupying power, and do a profitable sideline in extortion they're right on the bottom of everyone's Christmas present list.

It would be fascinating to know why Zacchaeus was attracted to Jesus. Idle curiosity, perhaps? Had he heard on the grapevine that Jesus befriended people like him? Then there was his tree-climbing. Was it just to get a better view, or did he want to hide his interest from general inspection? Maybe he wasn't sure himself. In some ways Zacchaeus is typical of many who might come to an all-age service. Not many would have a life of fraud to disguise, but they come with some burden they'd prefer to remain hidden. They probably come, too, because someone's told them about Jesus and they want to see for themselves.

Just like Bartimaeus and the demoniac, Zacchaeus changed immediately and dramatically. The evidence soon became clear when he went round to all the folk he'd overcharged, and repaid them – four times as much! C. S. Lewis once said that the last part of a man to be converted is his wallet. If it affects the cash flow, it must be genuine! No-one can argue about that kind of change. We can debate the nature of healings or even dismiss them as not genuine, but it's not possible to sneer at a changed lifestyle. The impact on Zacchaeus of his quite unexpected meeting with Jesus is a picture for us of how God can break into our most ingrained problems and make us new.

READINGS

2 Kings 5:1–14/2 Chronicles 33:1–13/ Jeremiah 18:1–10/Psalm 51/107:10–22/ Acts 16:16(or 22)–34/Romans 6:1–14/1 Peter 4:1–11/Matthew 9:9–13/Luke 5:1–11/19:1–10

HYMNS

Traditional

Jesus, thou joy of loving hearts
One there is above all others
Lord, speak to me, that I may speak
Master, speak, thy servant heareth
Come down, O love divine

Modern

Jesus, you are changing me
O let the Son of God enfold you
Set my spirit free
Jesus, take me as I am
O Lord, your tenderness

CONFESSION

Heavenly Father, we come to you with our burdens of sin and guilt. Forgive our reluctance to bring them before you, our refusal to open our lives to your searching gaze. Have mercy on us, Lord, and take away our heavy load. Bring us to yourself and restore us to your presence for the sake of our Saviour, Jesus Christ, Amen.

Almighty God, who forgives all who are open to receive his grace, have mercy upon you, pardon and deliver you from all your sin, strengthen you to do his holy will, and keep you in everlasting life through Christ our Lord, Amen.

INTERCESSION

Lord Jesus, you know us through and through because you made us. We can hide nothing from you, nor escape your light. Bless and guide your people through whom you shine. Make us lights for the world in our witness and service . . .
Light of the World,
Shine through us.

Lord Jesus, you know all things; nothing happens without your knowledge. Bless and guide all who govern the affairs of mankind. Make them lights for the dark places of this world . . .
Light of the World,
Shine through them.

Lord Jesus, you know pain and suffering; you lived in every respect as we do, yet without sin. Bless and comfort all whose lives are in distress. Make them aware of the light of your presence shining in their sorrow . . .
Light of the world,
Shine on them.

Lord Jesus, you know our weakness and frailty, yet you choose us as your servants and ambassadors. Bless and guide us in all we do, and make us lights for the world, reflecting your glory.
Light of the World,
Shine on us more and more until we see you face to face, Jesus Christ our Lord, Amen.

ALL-AGE ADDRESS

There are many ways of illustrating how God changes our lives when we allow him to. Stress that it's a total change, that something radical has happened. Younger children at least will know the toys called Transformers (so will their parents!). These are apparently toy cars, which when twisted around in certain ways can be turned into a robot. The best ones are so well constructed that it's almost impossible to tell that such a transformation is possible. This is a lovely picture of how we are the same, yet different, when God transforms our lives. But Zacchaeus didn't undergo a personality refit. He was still the same person. The change in his lifestyle was reflected by his actions. The same should be true of every Christian. We need to look, therefore, at *how* we've been changed, at where the difference is visible.

1) The first part of Zacchaeus' life to be affected when he met with Jesus was his fear. No longer did he need to pretend he wasn't there. John wrote in his first letter that 'perfect love casts out fear'. When we receive the love of Christ into our hearts it gets to grips with our fears, which are often the cause of our bad behaviour. A picture of someone quaking with fear could be shown at this point.

2) The second part was guilt. It's very important to distinguish between moral guilt and guilt feelings here, though the former may give rise to the latter. Zacchaeus had clearly done wrong. He was able to put it right, not by being especially brave but by recognising that he'd been forgiven and accepted by Jesus. A picture of a guilty look or act, such as taking a sweet furtively, will demonstrate what this means.

3) Finally, deal with Zacchaeus' relationships, which must have improved

almost infinitely! Because Jesus had removed his guilt and fear, Zacchaeus' problems with other people vanished. He felt confident about owning up to his wrongdoing and setting the record straight. Only Jesus can take away our fear and guilt. Such things are far too deeprooted for us to deal with on our own. To show this, use a picture of two people shaking hands or working together on something.

We don't need to be seriously ill or desperate for Jesus to change our lives – it's just that we often don't turn to him until such times. Other people shouldn't see only one time when we're transformed. It's a process that goes on throughout our lives as we grow more Christlike.

A useful resource for this service would be the song 'Oh! Zacchaeus!', No. 5 and 5a from the musical, *Singing Dancing Carpenter* by Michael Forster and Christopher Tambling, published by Kevin Mayhew.

A New Power

It may seem perverse to go to the book of Acts when the Gospels are so full of accounts of Jesus changing lives. This example doesn't directly involve Jesus, though he was certainly present as far as Peter and John were concerned. They were off to Evening Prayer as usual when they passed by a man begging at the Temple gate. No doubt he was there most days, trying to get a few coppers to keep him going. He couldn't walk so relied on others to get him there. Peter and John were pretty hard-up themselves, and hadn't brought any cash with them. So they couldn't help him financially. Instead they offered him the greatest gift of all. The ability to walk was obviously so precious to him that as soon as he realised what had happened he started dancing and leaping about and praising God very loudly. Not really British! It didn't suit the authorities either. They'd already been embarrassed about Jesus' body disappearing, so for his name and presence to be claimed for this miracle was doubly annoying.

Peter and John had no special training or qualifications, and they weren't officially recognised as having any spiritual authority. Yet their confidence in the risen Lord is such that they have no doubts about what they're to do. Peter doesn't just pray. He reaches down and hauls the man to his feet! Faith in action. Notice too how the former paralytic doesn't rush around saying how wonderful Peter and John are. He recognises that God has brought about this healing, and praises and worships him instead, not least with his newly-mobile legs.

The importance of this miracle isn't just that the power of the risen Christ is still available and as effective as it always was, but that those who follow him can call upon his Name and on that authority do as he did. Peter was the first to admit that he had no magic powers. It was the risen Christ working through him that made the man whole. God wants us, too, to exercise our faith in his Name, trusting wholly in him.

READINGS
Numbers 21:4–9/2 Kings 4:18–37/ Ezekiel 34:1–16/Psalm 62/103/Acts 3: 1–16/5:12–16/1 Corinthians 12:27–31/ Matthew 17:14–21/Luke 10:1–12/John 14:8–14

HYMNS
Traditional
O, for a thousand tongues to sing
Healing God, Almighty Father
Praise, my soul, the King of Heaven
Ye servants of God
Name of all majesty

Modern
Peter and John went to pray
His name is higher
Majesty
All hail, King Jesus
There is power in the name of Jesus

CONFESSION
Holy and immortal God, who raised your Son Jesus Christ from the grip of death to new and eternal life, we have not trusted in your power to heal and save. Our faith has been weak and our confidence lacking. Forgive us we pray, and by your Spirit make us firm in belief and bold in service for the sake of your Son, Jesus Christ our Lord, Amen.

God our Father have mercy on you, grant you forgiveness of all your sins, strengthen your faith in his power, and assure you of everlasting life through Jesus Christ our Lord, Amen.

INTERCESSION
Father God, mighty and powerful to save, we bring to you the concerns and needs of our world.
Lord of all hope,
Receive our prayers.

We bring to you the Church, both in our own country and throughout the world. Often disregarded and sometimes persecuted, your people still seek to bring the good news to those who've never heard it. We pray for this church . . . We also remember the church in other places . . .
Lord of all hope,
Receive our prayers.

We bring to you the whole world, with all its anguish and unhappiness. Despite the obstacles, relief is still being brought to those in desperate situations. We pray for our own country, and the governments of the world . . .
Lord of all hope,
Receive our prayers.

We bring to you our friends and members of our community who have a special need of your healing touch. Some are forgotten and lonely, some are grieving and sorrowful, others are unwell and in pain. We pray for any known to us . . .
Lord of all hope,
Receive our prayers.

We bring you ourselves, not only in church but wherever we are, in school, at work, with our friends and neighbours. May we extend to them your healing hand, that they may know you making them whole.
Lord of all hope,
Receive our prayers for the sake of Jesus Christ our Lord, Amen.

ALL-AGE ADDRESS
The vital point about this narrative from the book of Acts is that Jesus himself wasn't physically present, yet so confident were Peter and John of his power at work that they appear to have had no hesitation in offering healing to this person. Apart from their time with Jesus, they'd had no formal training in the healing ministry. All they could do was go ahead in faith. The authorities' question to them is revealing – "By what power or what name did you do this?" The whole account is held together by the name of Jesus; in a chapter and a half, it's mentioned nine times. We are only able to minister in this way if we do so in Jesus' name – i.e. on his authority. This can be illustrated in several ways.

1) There's an authority which entitles us to go. Here you could produce a passport or a railway ticket. The former authorises the holder to cross national boundaries (in the name of the rulers of the country) and the latter indicates that payment has been made for a journey by train, allowing the bearer to get on board.

2) There's an authority which entitles us to represent. A police officer is a good example of this, so if you have one in your congregation try to persuade him or her to appear in uniform. Otherwise, an OHP slide or flipchart diagram will do well. Police officers represent the forces of law and order. Merely by walking or driving around the patch, they are visibly acting as such.

3) There's an authority which entitles us to do something. A nurse or doctor is a very good example of this – and

again, a co-operative member of the congregation will prove an excellent and easily prepared visual aid! The alternative of a picture is less dramatic and unable to interact, but makes the point perfectly well. A nurse's uniform or a doctor's white coat are an indication that they're able to do certain things to our bodies which no-one else can. They've been trained, and have certificates to prove it (if these can be brought in as well, so much the better!).

All these points can be used as a parallel with God's authority to us to act in his name. We have his authority to go wherever he calls us. It's important to be sure that this is truly what he wants. We also represent him to other people. Jesus is back in Heaven with his Father, but the Holy Spirit within us not only helps us recognise where God may be calling us, but also helps others see the power of God at work in our lives. As his ambassadors we have his authority to speak on his behalf and to share his good news with others. We can also act in Jesus' name. If we try to live the Christian life any other way we'll fail. Only when we do his will do we have his authority, however. God wants all who follow him to serve him, but not by doing whatever they think of first. He'll make it plain what we're to do and give us strength to do it. When we know we're acting in Jesus' name and with his authority, it increases our confidence tenfold.

A New Faith

There are few more dramatic stories in the Bible than the conversion of Saul. It's always been regarded by the Church as a key event and is celebrated each January 25th. Unlike the other four characters in this section, whose lives were changed by Jesus, Saul had little idea that much was wrong with his life. On the contrary, few people seemed more convinced of their own rightness than Saul. He persecuted early Christians, not because he was a thug or a demagogue, but because he sincerely believed that he was right and they were wrong. Since he had a superb mind, he'd no doubt worked out all the answers against the Christian faith, just in case anyone challenged him. On the day he set out for Damascus he had no inkling that by the end of it he'd be a Christian himself.

In one moment the self-righteous zealot who'd willingly kill those who disagreed with him, was floored by an encounter with the risen Lord. All his bigotry and prejudice, all his arguments and intellect, were cut through in an instant. It was just as remarkable a change as Zacchaeus giving his money away, Bartimaeus walking around without bumping into things, the man at the Temple leaping around and praising God, or the demoniac in the Synagogue behaving normally. Saul's companions must have been lost for words!

That Paul regarded this turning point as a direct meeting with Jesus is beyond any doubt. What actually changed in Paul? His self-righteousness and intellectual arrogance vanished and instead his mind was turned to putting the Christian faith into a reasoned theology. Without his letters, our understanding of the Christian faith would be much the poorer. He was also willing to give God control of his life, not something he'd have found easy, and as a result committed his life to preaching the good news of Jesus. He probably remained an austere, rather prickly figure, but the very things in his make-up that had led him into persecuting Christians became the elements which God transformed into the leading apologist for the faith in the Early Church, if not of all time. Even Saul, to his amazement (and the consternation of everyone else!) couldn't resist the power of this encounter. Even if most Christians today don't experience quite the same vision, they can still know the power.

READINGS
Exodus 3:1–12/Judges 6:11–24/Isaiah 6:1–8/Psalm 22:22–31/73:13–28/107: 17–22/Acts 9:1–19/26:9–18/Galatians 1:11–24/Matthew 19:27–30/Mark 8:31–9:1/Luke 9:28–36

HYMNS
Traditional
Jesus, the very thought of thee
And can it be
To God be the glory
I will sing the wondrous story
I heard the voice of Jesus say

Modern
All the riches of his grace
Meekness and majesty
I am a new creation
Jesus, we celebrate your victory
The price is paid

CONFESSION
Risen Lord Jesus, we confess to you the sins and failings which keep us from you. We are sorry for the wrong we have done and said, and the wrong in our hearts which causes us to sin. Have mercy on us, pardon our offences, and by your Holy Spirit

break into our hearts with your risen presence. Turn us back to you and make us worthy servants of your eternal kingdom, where one day we will see you face to face, Jesus Christ our Lord, Amen.

God our Father by his great mercy forgive you all your sins, release you from guilt and shame, and restore you to his service for the sake of Jesus Christ our Lord, Amen.

INTERCESSION
Let us pray that the light of the risen Christ will break through in our hearts and in the world, as we say:
Break into our lives, Lord Jesus,
And grant us your peace and joy.

Risen Christ, break into the affairs of mankind. Transform by your power the suffering and injustice, the fear and despair. We pray for those in war-torn and tension-ridden areas . . .
Break into their lives, Lord Jesus,
And grant them your peace and joy.

Risen Christ, break into the wickedness and corruption around us. Transform our society by your power and work through our government to bring justice and peace to everyone. We pray for those in authority . . .
Break into our nation, Lord Jesus,
And grant us your peace and joy.

Risen Christ, break into your Church. Transform by your power the disunity and division, the apathy and fear. We pray for our witness to those around
. . .
Break into your Church, Lord Jesus,
And grant us your peace and joy.

Risen Christ, break into the lives of our families and friends. Transform by your power the situations of illness, grief and anxiety. We pray in particular for . . .
Break into their lives, Lord Jesus,
And grant them your peace and joy.

Risen Christ, break into our lives, transform our hearts and minds and make us new by the power of your Spirit. Hear our prayers and answer them as you know best in the name of Jesus, Amen.

ALL-AGE ADDRESS
The aim of this address is to demonstrate how when God breaks into our lives he takes full control. As a visual aid the ideal is a remote-controlled model car, which gives you control over speed, stopping and steering. It's important to use this as a parallel with a real car. First, ask what would happen if a car set off without a driver. Somebody will point out the likelihood of a crash soon after! A moving car is lethal unless someone is in control of it. Using the model indicate that the driver needs to know how to stop the car once it's started, how to guide the car in the right direction, and how to adjust the speed. This could be reinforced with OHP or flip-chart diagrams, which would be the alternative to a model if none were available.

Use these three points to draw a parallel with Paul. Before God broke through in his life, he was dangerous, certainly to the early Christians. He thought he was in control, but in reality the forces of darkness were running his life, as he later recognised. God took control and enabled him to stop behaving as he was, putting the brakes on Paul's persecution of Christians. He also took control of Paul's life so that he was going at God's speed, not at his own. Paul had to learn that the way he moved forward in his journey through life had to be determined by God. Finally God guided Paul on that journey, steering him through danger, crisis and opposition as he preached the good news in many areas which had never previously heard it. You could perhaps mention the 'Macedonian vision' as an example of the Holy Spirit guiding Paul in the right direction. Unlike a car, which has no mind, we can take a decision whether to allow God to take control.

We must also come under God's control if we are to stop behaving in wrong ways, to move on in our pilgrimage, and to go in the right direction. We can do none of this on our own. Only with God in control by his Holy Spirit are we able to serve him as Paul did.

Parables

Throughout the history of the Christian church, Jesus' parables have exerted an extraordinary influence. Challenging, inspiring, thought-provoking, they pack as powerful a punch today as they ever did. Over the centuries there have been innumerable attempts to interpret and reinterpret them, and their riches still seem inexhaustible. For an all-age service they offer ideal material – a story, a moral, a picture or puzzle. The early Church Fathers, especially Augustine, tended to allegorise the parables out of existence. They became so laden with meaning that Jesus' original point was quite obscured. It's a trap best avoided. The beauty of these brilliant pictures lies in their utter simplicity. As is so often the case, the simplicity reveals their profundity. Each parable offers so much potential that no address could begin to do it justice. However, a few suggestions are contained in this section, with the aim of trying to uncover what Jesus is saying through them to us, who live 2000 years later. The simpler the approach, the more likely this is to be achieved.

The Great Banquet

This is Jesus at his most entertaining. No further proof could be needed of Jesus' sense of humour! His wit cuts like a rapier through the veneer of religious hypocrisy which surrounded him, and puts the final banquet at the end of the age into a totally different light. The concept of God bringing all things together at the last day in a glorious feast was one that Jesus' hearers would have been familiar with (see, for example, Isaiah 25:6–9). It seems, however, that some of his contemporaries had become very status-conscious about it. There was at least an assumption that not everyone was invited. As he did frequently, Jesus overturns completely the popular ideas, in this instance about God's Kingdom.

The parable was told in response to a particularly pious remark from a holier-than-thou individual who was trying to make an impression on Jesus. His observation was true enough, but he hadn't understood what Jesus' mission was about. Jesus is answering the unspoken question about who will be invited to this wonderful feast. It's quite clear that nobody will be excluded from receiving an invitation, but not everyone will accept. The excuses that are made are ludicrous. Whoever declines such an offer to cultivate a field or look after animals? And why would marriage prevent it? Jesus is underlining the absurdity of the situation, and parallelling it with the refusal of the Jews to accept him or his message of good news. Instead of those who turned the invitation down, the poor and the rejected are given the opportunity to come and enjoy the feast. All those who would have been despised by the original invitees are now to be found at the table. It won't be the pious and religious types who sit down there, but the sort of people Jesus mixed with. They didn't make excuses or find other things to do, but received the offer gladly and were welcomed in. There are plenty of twentieth century excuses for ignoring Jesus, which need pointing out. This is an excellent theme for a Eucharistic service, as all are invited to the altar to share in the bread and wine which are a foretaste of the feast we'll enjoy one day in God's Kingdom, if we accept his invitation.

READINGS
Deuteronomy 26:1–11/Isaiah 25:6–9/ 55:1–5/Psalm 23/36/1 Corinthians 11:20–34/Revelation 21:1–7/22:1–6/ Luke 14:15–24/22:14–30/John 6:41–58

HYMNS
Traditional
We come as guests invited
The King of love my shepherd is
The Lord's my shepherd
My God, and is thy table spread
Bread of Heaven, on thee we feed

Modern
The trumpets sound
I am the Bread of Life
This is the feast of victory
Broken for me, broken for you
Seek ye the Lord, all ye people

CONFESSION
Eternal Father, you have graciously invited us to share in your Kingdom, but we have turned you down. Forgive our rejection of your love and resistance to your initiative, and pardon our self-reliance. Bring us back to the foot of the Cross and restore us to the fellowship of your table for the sake of your Son, our Saviour Jesus Christ, Amen.

Almighty God, who forgives all who

truly repent, have mercy on you, pardon and deliver you from all your sins, confirm and strengthen you in all goodness, and keep you in life eternal through Jesus Christ our Lord, Amen.

INTERCESSION
Heavenly Father, you invite us to your eternal banquet, not because of our virtue, but because you want us there.
Generous God,
Make us one with you.

Heavenly Father, you have called us with all Christian people to be members of your Kingdom. We pray for the Church throughout the world, as well as here . . . Help us to live out the unity you died to bring about between us.
Generous God,
Make us one with them.

Heavenly Father, there is room in your Kingdom for the poor, the homeless, the oppressed and the unwanted. We pray for all whose experience of the world causes them pain and suffering . . . Help us to show them your compassion.
Generous God,
Make us one with them.

Heavenly Father, we pray for your Kingdom to come in places of hardship, distress, war and fear, especially . . . Help all who seek to bring relief or peace in these situations.
Generous God,
Make us one with them.

Heavenly Father, the light of your Kingdom shines in every kind of darkness. We pray for all who are in need of your healing touch on their

lives . . . Help them to know your love and care.
Generous God,
Make us one with them.

Heavenly Father, keep us firm in our faith and sure in our hope as we live for you on earth. We pray that in our lives your Kingdom will come and your will be done . . .
Generous God,
Make us one with you both now and in the world to come when we will enjoy your presence for evermore, Amen.

ALL-AGE ADDRESS
Invitations make for a good all-age address. You'll need to prepare two large invitation cards, visible to the whole congregation. The first is to a low-quality meal. If possible, try to include in the wording some indication of how awful it will be. Tempting dishes on offer could be 'washing-up-water soup', 'fat-and-gristle pie', 'overcooked vegetables' and 'sour rhubarb with lumpy custard'. You may like to translate these into something impressively French, which you can then translate back again! The important factor is to ensure that nobody would want to accept such an invitation. Cap it all by saying that every guest will have to pay a hundred pounds for the pleasure, and then ask who wants to attend. It's not too hard to get a 100% negative response!

Then produce a second invitation, less impressively presented but with a much more mouthwatering menu. Smoked salmon, caviar, syllabub . . . whatever sounds delicious and exotic should be mentioned, so that the prospect is appealing. If there are lots of children, their favourite food might also be 'available' – chicken nuggets, Big Macs, crisps etc. Conclude sadly by stating that it will cost the guests nothing at all, and ask who wants to go. The response should be clear.

Jesus' invitation to the 'banquet' in Heaven is better than anything we can imagine here on earth, and costs us precisely nothing. If we reject his generosity we don't know what we'll be missing. Many people think that there can't be anything better than what we enjoy here and now, but those who follow Jesus can have a foretaste of how much better Heaven will be. Nobody sensible would turn down a good offer like that. Yet we carry on making excuses which are as silly as the ones in Jesus' parable – "I haven't got time", "I'm not really interested", "I've got other priorities", "my work and family are more important". Finish by emphasising how good God's invitation is and that all we have to do is respond to him in faith.

The Talents

In the context of this parable the talent is a large amount of money (in twentieth century terms several thousand pounds, maybe a year's salary); originally it was a weight. It's got little to do with our natural abilities or gifts. There are plenty of people who use their individual talents to great effect, but wouldn't claim to be Christians, though God certainly wants us to use these gifts for his glory.

The point of the parable is clear enough. The amounts given to each employee are of no consequence to their boss; he's more interested in what they've done with it. That Jesus was aiming this at the Pharisees and religious leaders is evident from the context. They were the guardians of the Torah (the Law) and in the tradition of that time they preserved it, unchanged and unsullied by ordinary people. They wanted a relationship with God that involved no change and no risk. They wanted to be in control of it, and of God. As leaders of God's people they had responsibilities, but they weren't willing to discharge them. Far from being a faith community Israel had become dominated by legislation and religious red tape.

Faith involves risk. Moving forward with God involves change. The whole history of Israel was based on faith, from Abraham, through Moses and Joshua to the prophets. Religion that's comfortable and easy may make us feel good but it hasn't got much to do with the Christian faith. The trouble is, it doesn't satisfy for long. We're all given responsibilities by God and one day he'll ask us to account for how we've exercised them. The man who came under judgement did so because he'd taken the safe option, under the wrong impression about his master. We'll hear our Lord say "Well done, good and faithful servant" not by staying where we

are, but by trusting God and going forwards. As John Wimber says, faith is spelt R-I-S-K.

READINGS
Numbers 13:26–33/Nehemiah 4:1–9/ Habakkuk 2:1–5/Psalm 18:20–28/ 37:23–31/97/Romans 1:8–17/ 2 Corinthians 5:1–10/2 Thessalonians 1/Matthew 24:42–51/25:14–30/Mark 11:20–25

HYMNS
Traditional
Teach me, my God and King
Take my life and let it be
Fill thou my life, O Lord my God
Lord of all power, I give you my will
Forth in the peace of Christ

Modern
Let us talents and tongues
Lord, make me an instrument
Seek ye first the Kingdom of God
I want to worship the Lord
All earth was dark

CONFESSION
Lord Jesus, we repent of our faithlessness and doubt and ask you to help our unbelief.
In your great mercy,
Lord, forgive us.

Lord Jesus, we repent of our self-will and pride and ask you to deal with our arrogance.
In your great mercy,
Lord, forgive us.

Lord Jesus, we repent of our stubbornness and refusal to change, and ask you to heal our insecurity.
In your great mercy,
Lord, forgive us.

Lord Jesus, we repent of all that prevents us from following you in faith, and ask you to make us loyal and trustworthy servants for the sake of your glorious Kingdom, Amen.

INTERCESSION

Heavenly Father, Master of all, we ask you to help us take seriously the responsibilities you give us. May we be responsible members of your Church . . . May we be responsible citizens of the world . . . May we be responsible carers of those who are in need . . . May we serve you faithfully in all you call us to do, that we may hear you say one day, "Well done," and enter into your eternal joy for Jesus Christ's sake, Amen.

Lord Jesus, our faith is not great. We feel small and uncertain, lost without you. Yet even though our faith is no larger than a mustard seed nothing is impossible with you. Help us to see you at work in our own lives as you lead us forwards, and guide us on our journey through life. Increase our faith and make us bold to work for your Kingdom whatever the cost, for the sake of our Saviour Jesus, who died for us and now lives forever, Amen.

ALL-AGE ADDRESS

This parable is easily distorted to fit in with the British idea of 'doing our best'. That isn't wrong unless it becomes the means of salvation, but it isn't really what Jesus is saying. The first part of the talk addresses the wrong concepts of God which many have, and which caused the wicked servant to be dismissed from his Master's presence. On an OHP slide have a picture of a police officer looking very stern. Ask if anyone is worried by the sight of a police officer or patrol car, and then explain that some people see God like that, a forbidding figure who's watching for every false move we make and noting it down to be used in evidence against us. The next picture is of a judge, looking angry and waving his finger accusingly. Find out if anyone would like to face this judge, and then show how some people think God is an angry judge, who can't wait to throw us into prison for ever. The final picture is of Santa Claus. Since everyone will love him, you need to say quickly that God isn't like Santa, who does nothing except give presents. Move into the second part of the address by saying that if we know God we'll find out what he's like – loving and gentle but pure and holy too.

For this part of the sermon you'll need a packet of seeds and the type of plant they'll grow into. Geranium seeds are useful because they're also quite small, and geraniums are easily obtained at any time of year. You'll need, too, a small pot full of compost. Ask someone to take a look at one seed and see if they can identify it. Will it grow, or are you having them on? Once they've ascertained that it's a seed, get them to place it in the pot full of compost. After a few seconds point out that it isn't growing. This may provoke some feedback, but then say that although it takes ages, sooner or later that seed will grow into a beautiful plant (here produce the bloom in question). God gives us seeds of faith, and it's our responsibility to plant and nurture them. If we don't plant the seed and let it grow, we'll still have a lovely packet, but no beautiful flowers. If we don't use our faith, take a risk and give it a chance to grow, our lives will never bear fruit. We may feel our faith is really small, that God can't do anything with it, but if we trust him and are willing to move forwards with him, it will be transformed, like the seed, into something infinitely bigger and better.

The Prodigal Son

Strictly speaking this parable is about the lost son, coming as it does in the context of a lost sheep and a lost coin. His use of his father's cash was certainly prodigal, but the point is that to the father his son was lost. Under Jewish law he was entitled to claim his share of the inheritance, probably remaining answerable for his use of it, however. The father, whether through choice or necessity, didn't call his son to account. Given all this freedom, the son went off and lived it up. Not surprisingly, his resources soon ran out and before long he hit rock bottom – what could be worse for a Jew than mucking out pigs and sharing their food? So he returns, and the focus moves to his father, who's been waiting for this moment ever since the son left. There's no demand for an explanation, no reluctance to receive this sad and forlorn figure, no request for reimbursement, and no requirement to make restitution. In fact, he's received back with open arms and given a royal welcome. Jesus wants us to see what his Father is really like, not a grumpy constable, or a cold law official, but loving and forgiving of those who turn back to him. There are no conditions to be met, no humiliation or dressing-down.

But although all Christians would assent to this, many still see God as a distant angry deity and find it hard to conceive of him as a loving Father. And unlike God, the Church has frequently made all sorts of demands on those who wish to join it that Jesus never made. Like the older son, the Pharisees had got totally the wrong idea about God. Grace and love were alien to their understanding. As a result they made unfair and ludicrous demands on the people. Jesus rectified that misunderstanding for many. He shows us the scope of the Father's love and his willingness to receive us back, however far we may have fallen. But he shows us too that we all too easily adopt the older son's mentality and become resentful when God doesn't fit into our preconceived idea of how things should be.

READINGS
2 Chronicles 30:1–9/Jeremiah 3:14–18/ Hosea 6:1–6/Psalm 51:10–17/71:14–24/ 81:8–16/Romans 8:12–17/Ephesians 4:1–6/1 John 2:28–3:10/Matthew 7:7– 12/Luke 15:11–32/John 15:9–17

HYMNS
Traditional
Father of Heaven, whose love profound
Come, let us sing of a wonderful love
Jesus, thou joy of loving hearts
Father, Lord of all creation
Great is thy faithfulness

Modern
Father God, I wonder
Father in Heaven, how we love you
Father, we adore you
Hallelujah, my Father
I'm accepted, I'm forgiven

CONFESSION
Let us return to the Lord our God and say to him:
Father, we have sinned against heaven and against you. We are not worthy to be called your children. We turn to you again. Have mercy on us, bring us back to yourself as those who once were dead but now have life through Christ our Lord, Amen. (Luke 15)

May God our Father forgive you your sins, and bring you to the fellowship of his table with his saints for ever, Amen.
(from *Patterns for Worship*)

INTERCESSION
Loving Father, your arms are
outstretched to embrace all who turn
back to you. Hear us as we pray,
saying:
Father of all mercies,
Hear us as we call.

Loving Father, your arms are
outstretched to support and uphold all
who own your name. We pray for the
Church . . .
Father of all mercies,
Hear us as we call.

Loving Father, your arms are
outstretched to save and redeem those
whose lives are spoiled by fear and ill-
treatment, poverty and violence. We
pray for . . .
Father of all mercies,
Hear us as we call.

Loving Father, your arms are
outstretched to touch and heal those
who suffer through illness, anxiety or
sadness. We pray for . . .
Father of all mercies,
**Hear us as we call, and answer our
prayers as you know is best, for the
glory of Jesus Christ our Lord, Amen.**

ALL-AGE ADDRESS
What Jesus most wanted his hearers to
understand from this parable was the
extent of his Father's love, and the lack
of any small print in his acceptance of
those who return to him. They're
welcomed, like the lost son, with open
arms and a celebration. It's such a
wonderful story that further illustration detracts from it. It's also worth
noting that portraying our heavenly
Father's love runs into difficulty with
those whose concept of being fathered
is damaged or embittered.

This idea requires four OHP slides
or flip-chart drawings. There are two
points of focus, the first of which is the
son. The two pictures show his disre-
gard of other people and their feelings, and his delusion that money
could buy him happiness.

The first should have him drawn at
the centre of a crowd, larger than the
other figures. He is smiling but they're
in the background with sad expressions. Point out how this young man
was indifferent to the pain and sadness he caused his father, and to the
anger and bewilderment of the rest of
the household. Make a parallel between this and our own indifference to
the suffering of so many in our world.
Even as Christians we're often more
concerned with our comfort and
security than with sharing or alleviat-
ing the pain experienced by others.

The next picture should have him
surrounded by fast cars, glamorous
women and bottles of wine or champagne. The younger son thought he
could use his inheritance to buy happiness. All he achieved was a tempor-
ary jollity. Point out the difference
between true happiness and enjoying
a party. God isn't a killjoy but he's
made us so that only in relationship
with him will we be truly happy. If we
look elsewhere in this world to find
security and contentment we'll be
sadly disappointed. No wonder there
are so many sad people around!

The other two pictures focus on the
father. The first portrays him handing
over a cheque or a wadge of banknotes
to his son. Explain that the father was
willing to allow his son the freedom to
go off and do his own thing. By his
attitude the son showed that he
couldn't handle that kind of responsibility. Sad though his father was, he

let him go. God gives us that kind of freedom, to choose whether to stay with him or go our own way. We have to own the responsibility for the way we live. The second picture shows the father welcoming his long-lost son home. Unlike the older brother, their father has no reservations about allowing his errant offspring back into the family – even the younger son himself expected to be taken on only as a hired hand on the farm! He's still loved and he's still the son, and a huge party is thrown in honour of his homecoming (you could also have a picture of this if desired). God makes us part of his family without any strings attached. There are no conditions to meet and no-one is too bad to be accepted. However awful we may think we are, our heavenly Father is still more than ready to forgive us and receive us back. The only person who didn't end this story happy ever after was big brother, who resented the attention given to his delinquent sibling. As Christians we must welcome others into God's family as our heavenly Father does, without conditions or reservations.

The Pearl of Great Price

None of Jesus' parables could be described as lengthy, but this is about the shortest. It may not be a beautiful and self-contained short story like the Prodigal Son, but it strikes at the heart of our priorities and values. Few things give away more about us than what we spend our money on. It creates more than anything else the image we have of ourselves and what we want other people to think of us. Every week in the Sunday Times there are advertisements for 'special' car registration plates, some of which sell for six-figure sums. Even if I had that much spare cash I can't see myself buying a number plate with it! Yet for some people that's an important part of their image. I'd rather use the car to show off my wealth – a Jaguar would do well. Others prefer to spend lavishly on clothing. There are antique collectors, sports enthusiasts – we all express in our spending what we value most, however much or little we may feel we have.

Although often quoted as a twentieth century invention, materialism is hardly new – look at the book of the prophet Amos. Wealth is a very unreliable source of security, however, and when unemployment is on the increase and inflation rising, people soon start to look elsewhere to find their values. The phenomenal rise in the value of antiques indicates an insecurity in the present which expresses itself in an urge to preserve the past – or rather a rose-tinted version of it. Alternatively the rise of the New Age movement and interest in Eastern religions suggests a dissatisfaction with what might be called 'traditional western values'.

Jesus wanted his hearers to see that the only place worth putting our treasure, or values, is in God's Kingdom. Our enjoyment of this life is enhanced by seeing it in the perspective of eternal life, a message desperately needed by so many today.

READINGS
Genesis 13·1–11/Joshua 1:6–9/Isaiah 55:1–5/Psalm 16/84/146/1 Corinthians 3:10–17/2 Corinthians 9:6–15/ 1 Timothy 6:3–10/Matthew 6:25–34/ 13:44–46/Luke 12:13–21

HYMNS
Traditional
My God, how wonderful thou art
Crown him with many crowns
Give to our God immortal praise
Glorious things of thee are spoken
Praise to the holiest in the height

Modern
Lord, you are more precious than silver
Worthy art thou
Worthy, O worthy are you, Lord
Come and praise him, royal priesthood
I want to thank you, I want to praise you

CONFESSION
Lord God, you are the Holy One, enthroned in splendour. You are rich beyond all telling, yet we have remained in poverty by neglecting you. Forgive our sinfulness and short-sightedness, we pray, and help us to see past the things of this world to your eternal Kingdom and there to put our treasure for the sake of your Son, Jesus Christ our Lord, Amen.

God, our merciful Father, whose mercy knows no bounds, grant you pardon and deliverance from all your sins, freedom from the chains of this world, and the riches of his glorious Kingdom, through Christ our Lord, Amen.

INTERCESSION
Lord Jesus, who left the riches of
Heaven and for our sake became poor,
hear us as we seek your face, saying:
Lord, may we seek first your
Kingdom,
And find in you our treasure.

Lord Jesus, help us not to become
submerged by the rising tide of
materialism, but to stand out as those
whose treasure is in Heaven. May the
Church be salt for our society as we
bear witness to that which lasts
forever. Especially we pray . . .
Lord, may we seek first your
Kingdom,
And find in you our treasure.

Lord Jesus, help us not to be
conformed to this world, but to be
transformed by your renewing power.
May we be citizens of our land, but
ambassadors for your Kingdom in the
darkness which surrounds us.
Especially we pray . . .
Lord, may we seek first your
Kingdom,
And find in you our treasure.

Lord Jesus, help us not to adopt the
values of the world but to bring it into
your will. May we share your love with
all who are ill or dying, anxious or
afraid, uncertain or despairing.
Especially we pray . . . Lord, may we
seek first your Kingdom,
**And find in you our treasure. Keep our
minds fixed on you until we meet you
face to face, and then forever, Amen.**

ALL-AGE ADDRESS
It would be easy to overload this
parable with twentieth-century examples and see it collapse under the
strain. Jesus wasn't condemning the
material world, or those who are wealthy. Wealth is a relative concept, de-
pending for its meaning on two things
being compared. Compared with
some of our neighbours we're hard
up, but set against many who live on
vast housing estates without employment or opportunity, many of us must
seem rich beyond belief. What Jesus
wants us to see is that his Kingdom is
far more valuable than anything this
earth can offer.

You'll need to display a selection of
objects of varying value. Priceless
antiques may be best left at home, but
there's a huge range of items which
could be included. It's most important
that you have at least a rough idea of
how much each is worth. Examples
might be a book (either 'coffee table'
or antiquarian), foods in packets or
tins (exotic or unfamiliar if possible)
and small household objects from the
kitchen or sitting room. Have a flip-
chart or OHP available and on a blank
sheet or acetate write up some of the
values which you ask the congregation
to estimate. Some at least will be
familiar with this idea from watching
the 'Antiques Roadshow' and gues-
sing at how much something might be
worth. The process shouldn't take too
long, or the point of the address will
be lost.

Move on to ask people what their
most prized possession is. You may
receive some surprising replies! Bring
out at this juncture something you
value highly, whether because of cash
or sentimental value. Would you get
rid of it for God's Kingdom? Say that
when you die you won't be able to
take it with you. God doesn't want to

spoil our lives by taking away everything we enjoy or treasure, but he
wants us to understand that his Kingdom is far more important than anything else. This world is beautiful, but
it can't last forever, unlike God's Kingdom. If we spend all our lives thinking
about this life only, we'll be far from
happy. But if we get our values sorted
out (which can be very hard) and put
God in first place, we'll be truly happy
and content.

The Sower

Jesus took as the subject matter for his parables scenes from everyday life, so it's hardly surprising that many of them refer to the natural world and growth. In this parable he takes the theme and develops it as far as he can. The explanation he gives to the disciples later certainly makes sense, but like all Jesus' parables it has several layers of interpretation. There are few things more satisfying than watching seeds germinate, grow and develop into flowers or vegetables. Even the least enthusiastic gardener can feel a sense of achievement when the dahlias come up through the surface of the soil for the first time, or when the first tomato is ready for harvesting. Despite modern city living, we haven't quite forgotten our rural roots! In drawing on this theme, Jesus is touching on something very profound within each of us.

Growth is a sign of life. A plant that isn't growing isn't alive. Children have to grow and even as adults we develop mentally and emotionally, though physical growth may have ceased. Here, Jesus makes that plain. The seed scattered by the farmer lands on various types of soil, but only grows on one. Three lots germinate and start to grow, but two fail to become mature crops. As well as being a picture of how different people respond to the Gospel, it also depicts our own lives quite accurately. There are fruitful and fertile bits in all of us, but there are also stony places where nothing can grow, shallow areas where nothing can take root, and thorny patches where new shoots of growth are strangled. If we're to grow spiritually, the seed of God's love needs to take root in the right soil, which is a heart warmed by God's love, dug over by the Holy Spirit, and nourished by his word. Many never enter the Kingdom, or start to grow in this way, because the 'seed's' landed where it won't grow. As Christians we often find areas of our lives which remain unaffected by God's work.

God wants mature crops from his seed. Once we've started to grow in our faith, we keep on growing. This becomes more important as time goes on. If the process stops, something has gone wrong. Both as individuals and churches we need to check that there's continuous growth and development, preparing us for eternal life.

READINGS
Proverbs 3:1–10/Isaiah 5:1–7/ Zechariah 8:9–19/Psalm 1/52/92/ 1 Corinthians 3:1–9/Ephesians 4:11– 16/Colossians 1:3–14/Matthew 13:1– 9(23)/Mark 4:26–34/Luke 8:4–15

HYMNS
Traditional
O breath of life, come sweeping
  through us
Breathe on me, breath of God
God made me for himself
For the fruits of his creation
Great is thy faithfulness

Modern
You are the vine
Colours of day
Give me oil in my lamp
I live, I live because he is risen
In my life, Lord

CONFESSION
Loving Father, we confess to you the many times when our lives have not borne fruit for your kingdom. We are sorry that your word falls on stony ground and never grows; that it falls on shallow soil and soon withers; that it falls on thorny ground and becomes choked. Pardon and deliver us we pray, and by your mercy grant that we

may be fruitful in your service to the glory of our Lord Jesus Christ, Amen.

God, who is rich in mercy, forgive you all your sins, heal you of all your infirmities and by his Spirit enable you to bring forth fruit for the sake of his Kingdom, through our Lord Jesus Christ, Amen.

INTERCESSION

Life-giving Lord, we bring to you our praises and requests as we say,
Lord of Life,
Receive your children's prayer.

We pray for our church, that we may grow together in faith and love . . .
Lord of Life,
Receive your children's prayer.

We pray for your people throughout the world, especially in places of fear, violence or hardship, that they may grow ever closer to you . . .
Lord of Life,
Receive your children's prayer.

We pray for those in authority, as they make many difficult decisions and seek to relieve suffering, that they may grow in wisdom and understanding . . .
Lord of Life,
Receive your children's prayer.

We pray for the lonely, the poorly, the elderly and the needy, that they may grow in their knowledge of your love . . .
Lord of Life,
Receive your children's prayer.

We pray for ourselves, that we may grow in faith and holiness, becoming more and more like Jesus.

Lord of Life,
Receive your children's prayer, and answer it for his Name's sake, Amen.

ALL-AGE ADDRESS

To illustrate this address you'll need a packet of seeds, some potting compost, a small amount of cement or sand, a couple of flowerpots, and either plants in various stages of growth or pictures of them. At the right time of year the appropriate flower or fruit could also be displayed to good effect.

Start by showing the congregation the packet of seeds and ask how to make them grow into flowers. The two points that should emerge are that the seeds need to be in the right soil and environment, and receive the appropriate care. Fill a flowerpot with some sand or cement and ask if that will do. When you receive the answer 'No', ask what's really needed, then fill another pot with compost, pushing a few seeds into it. Then ask what to do with it (make sure you read the instructions on the packet first so that you know!). Will it only germinate in the dark, or should it be put on a window sill, or even outside? And what treatment does it need? Watering daily, transplanting in May . . . ? Point out that things only grow properly in the right environment and with proper care. As Christians we need the environment of the church with other Christians to help our faith take root and grow well. And it needs to be watered and nurtured by constant contact with God through prayer and reading the Bible.

Now demonstrate either with the real thing or pictures the different stages of a plant's growth. The first stage is mostly unseen as the seed germinates below the surface and its roots form. Faith often starts unseen by anyone else. Then the first shoots appear and there are signs of life. This then develops more leaves and shoots until the plant is fully grown and ready to bear flowers or fruit. It doesn't achieve full growth overnight but takes time. So it is with our faith. Whether we become Christians suddenly or gradually, our faith grows throughout our lives and bears its fruit in due season. The closeness of our relationship with God and the evidence of our faith in the way we live are the fruits God requires of us. Finally, explain that when God speaks to us we can react in different ways. We can be like stony ground and not let it have any impact; we can be like shallow ground and not let it have any lasting effect; we can be like thorny ground, and not let it have any effect; or we can be fruitful ground that produces results for God's Kingdom.

The Holy Spirit Gives Us . . .

One of the most striking phenomena of the last twenty years in the Church's history has been the rise of the 'charismatic', 'renewal' or 'Pentecostal' movement. Every mainline church has been influenced by it to some degree. The Holy Spirit, who had previously been on the agenda for a small part of the year, suddenly became the centre of many churches' life and worship. Despite the popular conception of what 'charismatic' Christians are like, there's a huge variety of backgrounds and traditions within this worldwide movement, from Anglo-Catholic to Liberal, and through into Evangelical. Roman Catholic, Orthodox and 'High Church' charismatics happily meet with those from Lutheran, Methodist, Baptist and other free churches.

One of the most characteristic effects of this new openness to God's Spirit has been a much greater emphasis on his gifts to us and his effect on our lives. Churches which have experienced 'renewal' frequently have a strong ministry of the laity, and a willingness to relate to God directly over many areas of life. This section isn't based just on 1 Corinthians 12, but attempts to cover other areas which the Holy Spirit can bring to our lives. Many have experienced great blessing from God as a result of the renewing work of the Holy Spirit, but even churches that wouldn't call themselves 'charismatic' can benefit from this increased awareness of the Holy Spirit and how he can change our lives.

It's important to emphasise that the Holy Spirit never draws attention to himself, but always to Jesus Christ. His gifts aren't an end in themselves but the means whereby God enables and equips us to worship and serve him. Like every other teaching in the Church it needs to be rooted in an understanding of the Trinity. By definition the Holy Spirit operates more in the realms of our experience, but that shouldn't cut out the use of our minds. Feelings can be very unreliable!

The Holy Spirit Gives Us Peace

The English word 'peace', like its Greek counterpart 'irene', covers a range of meanings. Basically it implies an absence of noise or hassle; on a larger canvas it might mean an absence of conflict. But there's a deeper significance, too. Behind the absence of noise or warfare lies a tranquillity or serenity, and there are some people who convey that quality whatever may be happening around – an inner peace and confidence that enables them to ride out any passing storm. It isn't that something 'unpeaceful' is missing, but they can be positive whatever the situation. The Hebrew word 'shalom' sums this up. When a relationship or atmosphere is filled with God's peace it's made wholesome and good.

The Holy Spirit gives us that peace which passes all understanding. It doesn't need to be created or negotiated but received. Jesus, after his resurrection, comes to his frightened and troubled disciples in the upper room and says "Peace be with you," followed shortly after by "Receive the Holy Spirit." Only a few days earlier he'd promised them, "Peace I leave with you; my peace I give you." That's Jesus' promise to all who follow him. Not every Christian takes him up on this offer. Of course we can't be free of anxieties and concerns in this life, but they don't need to dominate and control our lives to the extent they often do. The Holy Spirit lives within all believers, but they may not be open to him being released in this way. The evidence of many Christians in difficult and dangerous situations is that they've been enabled to face conflict because of the Holy Spirit. They're not super-spiritual, but ordinary people transformed by him.

That same peace affects our relationships with one another, as well as with God. When we're not right with God we end up at sixes and sevens with each other. God's peace isn't just an inner 'feelgood' – its reality can be measured by the quality of our relationships. The wholeness that God wants all Christians to enjoy can transform not just our inmost thoughts, but also the outward expression of them. An African pastor who'd suffered terribly during the atrocities of the 1970's used to talk of 'peace-joy' as though these two were inseparable. He'd say "joy is peace dancing; peace is joy resting."

READINGS
Numbers 6:22–27/Proverbs 3:13–18/
Isaiah 32:14–20/Psalm 37:1–11/85/122/
Romans 4:13–19/Galatians 5:16–26/
Colossians 3:12–17/Luke 10:1–12/John 14:15–27/20:19–23

HYMNS
Traditional
Peace, perfect peace
Like a river glorious
The Lord's my shepherd
O love, that will not let me go
King of glory, King of peace

Modern
Peace I give to you
Peace is flowing like a river
My peace I give unto you
Peace to you
Make me a channel of your peace

CONFESSION
Almighty God, we confess that we have disobeyed your commands and not heeded your voice. We have lived for ourselves and not for you. Our hearts are not at rest and we need your peace. Forgive us, we pray, and deliver us from all our sins. Renew a right

spirit within us and grant us that peace which the world cannot give, which is the promise of Jesus Christ our Lord, Amen.

God our Father forgive you for all you have done contrary to his will and restore you again to the paths of peace which alone lead to eternal life, through Jesus Christ our Lord, Amen.

INTERCESSION
Lord Jesus, you promise us your perfect peace in this dark world of sin. We pray for that peace, saying:
Lord of Eternity,
Grant us your peace.

We ask for your blessing of peace upon our world, especially . . . So many places do not know peace, so many people live in hostility. Relieve all who suffer through violence and all who seek to bring an end to it.
Lord of Eternity,
Grant us your peace.

We ask for your blessing of peace on this church, especially . . . You died that all who believe in you might be one. Help us to live out our unity, reconciled to you and one another, bringing your reconciling power to a divided world.
Lord of Eternity,
Grant us your peace.

We ask for your blessing of peace on our families and friends, especially . . . May your peace be seen in all our relationships, in our homes and in our communities.
Lord of Eternity,
Grant us your peace.

We ask for your blessing of peace on those in need – the sick, the sad, the frail and the fearful, especially . . . You are our great high priest who shares in our suffering. Bless those we have named aloud and in our hearts with your healing touch.
Lord of Eternity,
Grant us your peace.

We ask for your blessing of peace. Help us to be open to your Holy Spirit, who brings us the peace of Christ. May our restless hearts find their rest in you alone.
Lord of Eternity,
Grant us your peace, and keep us in it as our minds remain fixed on you, through Christ our Lord, Amen.

ALL-AGE ADDRESS
'Shalom' really means 'wholeness', and it's that quality which God brings to us through the death and resurrection of his Son. Rather than discuss the nature of peace this sermon concentrates on the places where God's peace can operate, and on its effects.

1) In our hearts. On an OHP or flip-chart sheet draw some basic faces with various expressions – sad, angry, despairing, dejected, crying etc. Ask the congregation what might have happened to make them like that. Suggestions will probably include bereavement, upset, loneliness or suffering. Say that in this life many things happen to make us miserable at times. We can't help that, but God helps us to face those difficulties and keeps us from going under. If you know anyone who's an example of this you could tell their story at this point.

2) In our homes. Our homes aren't always very peaceful, and if we don't know God's peace within us, there's little chance of our relationships at home being totally peaceable. One way of depicting this would be a house with several people arguing or fighting. It can be extremely difficult getting along with those we're closest to, not least when we have to live under the same roof. Our relationships are fragile and easily damaged. When the peace of Christ enters our homes and hearts we're enabled to love one another and bear with each other as he does us.

3) In our community. What goes on in hearts and homes spills over directly into our community, however that is defined. A picture of a High Street, perhaps, with plenty of figures milling around, would make this point. It's easier in some areas than in others to demonstrate lack of peace in the community, but it's always possible to highlight other places, ideally not far away. Violence and fear are a real part of life for almost everyone, and the problem starts in our hearts and homes.

4) In our world. The world is made up of communities, small and large. The level of violence and conflict in the world today reflects what's happening in those communities. Hold up a globe at this point and point out how tiny each of us is in comparison to the size of the world. Yet the peace of the world depends first and foremost on individuals and homes knowing God's peace. Finally, emphasise the idea of the Church as an institution full of people, at peace with God and therefore each other.

The Holy Spirit Gives Us Faith

"If only I had your faith," people some-times say to me, assuming that the white plastic round my neck somehow imparts this quality to me in a way denied to other mortals. What exactly do they mean? Most are probably not sure, but if pressed would say it was something to do with an attitude to life, an 'optimism' or sense of certainty about the future, and maybe a greater conviction about 'morality'. It's very important to establish what we mean by faith as a gift from the Holy Spirit. Many people will think it's about 'believ-ing something very hard' or even 'believ-ing three impossible things before break-fast'. Others will equate it with a kind of naiveté.

Faith has several aspects, but in this context it isn't the faith in Christ which starts us on our Christian journey. Nor is it our creed or theological stance, though these certainly influence it. Faith is the consequence of having a right relationship with God and is based on our confidence in him. It's much easier, however, to identify it by its effects than by its nature. It's seen in the willingness to take a risk to achieve something for God's Kingdom. It's seen in the confidence that God will act in a given situation. It's seen in the commit-ment to Christian service that comes from a total conviction that God has called and equipped each individual for specific ser-vice in his name. Like all the Holy Spirit's gifts, faith isn't an end in itself. The Corinthian church ran into problems be-cause they were using these gifts for self-aggrandisement and personal kudos. God gives us faith so that we can serve him – and the more we use it the more we grow. Used for our own ends it goes sour on us; used for God's glory it achieves great things for him.

READINGS
Proverbs 28:20–29/Isaiah 12/Jeremiah 17:5–8/Psalm 9:1–10/56/86/Romans 1:8–17/Philippians 3:7–14/Hebrews 11:1–2 & 12:1–3/Matthew 8:5–13/17:14–20/Mark 7:24–30

HYMNS
Traditional
Have faith in God, my heart
How firm a foundation
A safe stronghold
Be thou my vision
We rest on thee

Modern
Jesus, we celebrate your victory
Praise the name of Jesus
We shall stand
Our confidence is in the Lord
You are my hiding-place

CONFESSION
Lord God, you are true and trustworthy. Your Word is utterly reliable. We are sorry and ashamed and repent of our faithlessness and sinfulness. Forgive us, we pray, and instil in us a true faith and sure hope, that we may put our confidence in you, the rock of our salvation and come at last to where you reign in glory with our Saviour, Jesus Christ our Lord, Amen.

Almighty God, who forgives all who truly repent, by his great mercy pardon all your offences, deliver you from the snares of evil, and set your feet in the way that leads to everlasting life for the sake of our Saviour Jesus Christ, Amen.

INTERCESSION

Lord God, you are our refuge and redeemer. We come before you with our prayers and requests, saying:
Faithful Lord, hear our prayer,
And keep us true to you.

We pray to you our shield and defender. Keep your guiding hand on your Church and protect her from evil and the distractions of the world as she seeks to proclaim your Kingdom. Especially we ask . . .
Faithful Lord, hear our prayer,
And keep us true to you.

We pray to you, our rock and strong fortress. Keep us in your care as we live day by day in this world, and help us to promote your love and justice wherever we have the opportunity. Especially we ask . . .
Faithful Lord, hear our prayer,
And keep us true to you.

We pray to you, our shelter and place of safety. Keep your loving touch on anyone we know who needs you as they endure sadness, loneliness, illness or unfairness. Especially we ask . . .
Faithful Lord, hear our prayer,
And keep us true to you.

We pray to you, our great high priest. Keep us in the way that leads to eternal life and increase our faith as we continue our earthly pilgrimage.
Faithful Lord, hear our prayer,
And keep us true to you for the sake of Jesus Christ, who died that we might live, Amen.

ALL-AGE ADDRESS

The objective of this address is to demonstrate how the Holy Spirit's gift of faith makes a difference to the way we live. It requires six drawings, either on OHP slides or on a flip-chart.

1) The first picture is of someone sitting at home, planning a journey. He may be holding a map, or looking at one fixed to a wall. Encourage the congregation to suggest where he might be going; the more exotic the destination the better. Choose a particularly glamorous one and emphasise how much this person wants to go there, just as we would. The trouble is, he's worried. Picture No. 2 shows him sitting in front of the TV. Although he'd love to make his journey he's afraid the plane will crash, that he'll be mugged, that he won't have enough money and that he won't be able to speak the language. Point out that if he wants to get there he must take the risk and go out. Faith is about going out confidently, believing God will protect and guide us. Unfortunately, many people 'stay at home' because they allow their fears to dominate their faith, and then regret that they don't seem to get anywhere spiritually.

2) The next two pictures demonstrate that faith not only goes out but goes forward. The first is of the same figure as before but walking backwards, looking over his shoulder. He isn't making much progress because all his thoughts are about where he's come from and where he's been. He isn't really looking where he's going and can't see ahead. The next picture shows him getting it right, striding out with some assurance about where he's heading. Explain that if we become obsessed with the past we'll never make progress into the future with

God. As pilgrims we're aiming to reach his eternal Kingdom, so we look ahead and go forwards in faith.

3) The final two drawings depict the same figure, first standing still, with a large hill in front of him. Ask why he's stopped, and pick on an answer which suggests he's finding the going a bit tough. The hill's steep and rough and he doesn't think he'll make it. Many Christians are like that – they start out on the journey but as soon as it gets more difficult they stop where they are. They can't face what comes next and wish they'd stayed at home. Finally show the figure on top of the hill, looking at the vista below him. He can enjoy the view because he's gone on in faith. We too must go on in our pilgrimage, not giving up or backing off when circumstances prove less easy than we thought. God's never promised us that the Christian life will be a pushover – far from it. But he has promised us his Holy Spirit to give us faith to go out in his name, vision to go forwards confidently, and strength to enable us to face the obstacles and hardships and overcome them as we journey through this life towards our eternal home.

The Holy Spirit Gives Us Healing

Of all the gifts of the Holy Spirit which have been 'rediscovered' by the Church, the gift and ministry of Christian healing is arguably both the most widely used and at the same time the most controversial. Churches of all traditions now have regular 'healing services', both 'high' and 'low', Catholic and Evangelical. Some prefer to associate healing with the sacrament, others open it on an ecumenical basis to members of other traditions. Yet although very many churches do now offer the ministry of healing, there are also a large number of Christians who have doubts about this aspect of the church's life, or whose misplaced hopes have been dashed. Unscrupulous operators have exploited people's vulnerability to make themselves a lot of money. There's an understandable fear of this ministry being abused for personal gain, and causing unnecessary pastoral problems.

It's important to recognise not only that God authorises his people to offer healing in his name, but also that we shouldn't become bogged down by physical healing. That certain individuals have received healing of a physical disease is beyond dispute. However, that doesn't entitle us to raise the hopes of every wheelchair-bound person that they'll automatically get up and walk away. There were times when Jesus wasn't able to heal many, and Paul had a condition which he longed to be released from, but had to endure as a 'thorn in the flesh'. In Jesus' ministry healing was also linked with preaching the Kingdom of God – it was a sign that God's Kingdom was at hand, that God was at work in the world.

Most healing prayer is directed not at the body but at the emotions and the soul.

In fact there are many instances of healing of the body resulting directly from prayer directed at the inner life. The emphasis should be away from spectacular miracles (though these should be acknowledged when they occur) and put instead on the way in which the Holy Spirit makes us whole, and helps us become the people God created us to be. That may involve dealing with events in the past, or anxieties in the present. It isn't God's will that we should be left in this life suffering agonies of doubt and fear, but that we should serve him in newness of life.

READINGS
2 Kings 5:1–14/Job 5:17–26/Jeremiah 17:12–18/Psalm 30/41/147:1–11/Acts 5:12–16/8:4–25/1 Corinthians 12:7–11/Matthew 12:22–32/Mark 3:1–12/Luke 7:1–10

HYMNS
Traditional
At even, 'ere the sun was set
Dear Lord and Father of mankind
O for a thousand tongues to sing
Praise, my soul, the King of Heaven
Healing God, Almighty Father

Modern
Praise you Lord, for the wonder of
   your healing
I believe in Jesus
You are the vine
The price is paid
I receive you

CONFESSION
We kneel before the Lord who heals us to confess our wrongdoing and sinfulness, as we say:
Merciful Father, create in us clean hearts,
And renew a right spirit within us.

We confess that we have done many things which are not in accordance with your laws. We have pursued selfish ends instead of following your way, and our lives have become lost and confused.
Merciful Father, create in us clean hearts,
And renew a right spirit within us.

We confess that we have spoken words which have hurt and caused unhappiness. We have not acknowledged you as Lord, but instead have allowed our tongues to run out of control.
Merciful Father, create in us clean hearts,
And renew a right spirit within us.

We confess that our hearts are full of wrong thoughts which issue forth in thoughtless deeds and Godless words. We have not allowed your power to transform our minds and hearts and they need healing.
Merciful Father, create in us clean hearts,
And renew a right spirit within us.
Make us whole in thought, word and deed, that our lives may glorify Jesus, who heals all who turn to him in repentance and faith, Amen.

INTERCESSION

Lord Jesus, Saviour and Healer, we pray that your healing touch will be extended to all who long for you to bring wholeness to their lives. You never turned away anyone who came to you to seek healing; you never rejected any who brought their pain to you in faith. We pray for those whose suffering is caused by poverty and deprivation . . . for those whose suffering is the result of violence and warfare . . . for those who suffer from neglect by the rest of society, the tramps, the drug addicts and the homeless . . . As you showed compassion to all who turned to you for healing, may we too, filled with your love, share your concern for the needy and helpless and in coming to their aid draw them into your loving embrace, for the sake of Christ our Lord, Amen.

Healing Father, we ask you to bless and make whole any known to us whose lives are spoiled by illness, anxiety or distress of any kind. Especially we pray for . . . May they know your love surrounding them, your grace upholding them and your power filling them, that their sorrows may fade away in comparison with the light of your presence as seen in your Son, our Saviour Jesus Christ, Amen.

ALL-AGE ADDRESS

If misunderstandings are to be avoided in the area of the Christian healing ministry, it's essential to use imagery not connected with the medical profession in any way. This address fixes on the concept of 'repairing', and as illustrations you'll need two identical cups or plates, one of which is broken (a jumble sale is often a good inexpensive source of such items); a battery-operated model or appliance, with the batteries removed; and a cut flower with a broken stem.

First take the model or appliance and demonstrate conclusively that it doesn't work – it's broken. Ask for help to put it right. Sooner or later somebody will mention batteries and you can produce the requisite number to make it work properly. It needed a new power source inside to become usable again. When God heals us it's as though he puts a new source of power inside us, to make us function as he intended. Often, things in the past prevent us from living as God meant us to. The Holy Spirit gives us healing to overcome this.

Secondly, take the flower and ask what you need to make it grow again. You may receive a few suggestions but ultimately a flower that's removed from its roots won't last very long. There's nothing we can do to repair it, and it's best thrown away. God never throws us to one side, however bad we may think we are. Jesus' harshest words were aimed not at the people who thought they were bad but at those who had a false idea of how good they were. No-one is beyond God's care and salvation.

Thirdly, take the broken plate/cup. Somebody will soon point out the need for instant glue (which you could produce if necessary). Demonstrate that the broken plate won't be quite what it once was, but can be put together very neatly so that no-one will recognise where it was damaged. It will be as usable and acceptable as the unbroken one. When God gives us his healing he makes us as though we'd never been broken. Unlike the glue, which may one day give way, God's love will hold us together forever. No healing can be more complete than Jesus', and he gives it to us for nothing. All of us long to be made whole, and wish we were less 'broken'. Jesus accepts broken people, and makes them whole once again.

The Holy Spirit Gives Us Gifts

It seems like a tautology to say that the Holy Spirit gives us gifts – anything given is by definition a gift. Yet Paul, along with the early church, recognised that apart from general blessings such as peace and healing there are also specific gifts, not given to all Christians, which are for the building up and nourishment of the whole church. In the letters to the Corinthians and Ephesians these are mentioned in the context of the Church as the Body of Christ. There's also a passage in Romans and 1 Peter, as well as an occasional reference in the book of Acts. It's clear that the lists of gifts given to those within the church are not exhaustive (each list is itself different from the others). God can equip us in any number of ways to serve him, both through our natural abilities and inclinations and through supernatural gifts which aren't connected with our personalities. It's a concept of the church which is a long way from the 'one-man-band' structure so familiar to western Christians.

If each member of the Body of Christ fulfils his or her function under the authority of Christ, the Head, the gifts of the Holy Spirit will be distributed so that no-one will be without, and no-one able to boast of their 'greater' gifts. The church at Corinth fell into all manner of traps over this, with the consequence that instead of the gifts being used to edify and build up, they were becoming a means of showing off and a political tool. If the gifts of the Holy Spirit are in evidence, so also should be his fruits.

Unfortunately, too much weight has been put on the 'spectacular' gifts such as healing, speaking in tongues and prophecy. As Paul had to point out, they're all bound together with love, and without it are of no consequence. For the majority of churches today there's little difficulty about the concept of 'every member ministry', in which all are encouraged to play as active a part as possible, using their particular gift from the Holy Spirit. This has to be co-ordinated but not suppressed. Every Christian has been given a particular gift by the Holy Spirit and is responsible for its proper use within the Body of Christ. The Body as a whole has to ensure that there is scope for those gifts to be exercised.

READINGS
Exodus 31:1–11/36:1–7/1 Samuel 18:5–16/Psalm 98/127/150/Romans 12:1–8/1 Corinthians 12:1–11/Ephesians 4:1–16/Matthew 25:14–30/Luke 21:1–4/John 14:1–14

HYMNS
Traditional
Come down, O love divine
Come, Holy Ghost, our souls inspire
Gracious Spirit, Holy Ghost
Holy Spirit, come confirm us
Come most Holy Spirit, come

Modern
Holy Spirit, we welcome you
My peace I give unto you
He that is in us
Spirit of God, unseen as the wind
Give me oil in my lamp

CONFESSION
Loving Father, you long to pour out your blessing upon us, and give us a foretaste of Heaven. We are sorry and ashamed that we have closed our eyes to your love, and have quenched the work of your Spirit. Forgive us, we pray, and open our hearts to receive

your gifts that we might rejoice to be called the children of God, through the love of your Son, Jesus Christ our Lord, Amen.

The all-merciful Lord forgive you for all your sins, grant you pardon and deliverance from all that is wrong and the grace and comfort of his Holy Spirit, through Christ our Lord, Amen.

INTERCESSION

Holy Spirit, you distribute gifts without partiality to all who follow Christ. Help us to receive gladly and employ willingly the gifts you have bestowed upon us.
Spirit of God, take our lives,
And fit us for your service.

Holy Spirit, grant to your Church the gifts of wisdom and discernment at a time of uncertainty and confusion. Help us all to work as one in you and act as salt in society. Especially we ask . . .
Spirit of God, take our lives,
And fit us for your service.

Holy Spirit, grant to the nations your gift of peace at a time of conflict and war. Help us to spread the good news of your Kingdom in the midst of darkness and despair. Especially we ask . . .
Spirit of God, take our lives,
And fit us for your service.

Holy Spirit, grant to those going through times of difficulty and pain your gift of healing as you know they need it. Help us to care for them as you care for us. Especially we ask . . .
Spirit of God, take our lives,
And fit us for your service. As we obey

your will may our hearts be gladdened, our faith strengthened and our souls uplifted through the love of your Son, Jesus Christ our Lord, Amen.

ALL-AGE ADDRESS

We receive gifts for many different reasons. Birthdays and Christmas come immediately to mind, but then we might think of 'thank you' presents, 'rewards' for an act of kindness or helpfulness, and 'I love you' presents. Surprise gifts like these are usually a great pleasure, though there can be one problem – what you receive isn't quite what you wanted. We feel slightly embarrassed to discover that we've got one of those already, or we're allergic to it, or we can't stand the colour! God's gifts to us come in three kinds – gifts expressed through words, gifts seen in actions, and gifts used in our thought processes.

1) Gifts which are connected with speaking include not only the gift of tongues and prophecy, but also teaching and evangelism. You could even mention the gift of being able to learn a foreign language to take the good news to other people. A good way to illustrate this is to display a dictionary. Explain that we don't need a huge vocabulary as far as God's concerned, because he will give us the words to say at the time we need them.

2) Gifts which are about 'doing' include healing and faith, but also pastoral care and practical help. Use simple household items such as a brush and dustpan to underline the point that God doesn't regard some gifts as better than others. Every task done to

God's glory for the benefit of the Body of Christ will receive his 'well done'.

3) Gifts which are active in the way we use our minds include knowledge and discernment as well as wisdom. A small hand-held computer is a good example to use. It can do very complex operations, probably faster than our brains can, but is limited by whatever is put in initially. It can only 'think' with the information it's given. Unlike us a computer can't discern or relate or love. God doesn't want to condition our minds but to work through them for his glory.

The Holy Spirit Gives Us Love

"Love is a many-splendoured thing" we're told. It certainly gets a great deal of attention, and lies at the heart of much of the world's greatest literature and drama. It's so basic to human relationships that there wouldn't be much interest or plot without it. It's also very complex. C. S. Lewis, in his book 'The Four Loves', identifies four different kinds of love – affection, friendship, eros and 'charity' (or in Greek 'agape', since we now use 'charity' in a rather different sense). There's nothing wrong with the other three, but the specific gift of the Holy Spirit to those who follow Christ is 'agape'. Regrettably society (and especially the media) focus almost exclusively on 'eros', forgetting that romantic and sexual love, wonderful gift of God as it is, only constitutes a part of love.

Paul is adamant that 'agape' love is the greatest of all the Holy Spirit's gifts. He goes so far as to say that without it, all the other gifts are worthless. In his great chapter on love, 1 Corinthians 13, he describes love in several ways, mostly by its effects, which were far from evident in the Corinthian church at that time. It isn't hard to boast about our gifts, but what really matters is whether the love of God is seen in our lives. The effects of love aren't seen in an occasional emotional spasm but in the ongoing willingness to put that into practice, day by day, regardless of any obstacles. Agape love is self-giving and sacrificial, not considering its own needs and aspirations but focusing entirely on the concerns of others. Supremely this love is seen in Jesus, who gave himself unstintingly even to the extent of dying on the Cross. Self-interest is completely absent from his life.

Most Christians will agree on the importance of love, but many churches find it hard to maintain loving relationships. In part this is because there's little understanding of love as an act of the will, but it's also due to our tendency to put our own interests on top of the pile and resist others who want to put theirs on top. If all we do is try to be loving we'll fail. Only as the Holy Spirit fills us with the love of Jesus will we be able to demonstrate that love in our own relationships.

READINGS
Deuteronomy 7:7–11/Isaiah 43:1–7/ Hosea 3/Psalm 86/92/136:1–9/Romans 13:8–12/1 Corinthians 12:31–13:13/ 1 John 4:16b–21/Mark 12:28–34/Luke 6:27–36/John 15:9–12

HYMNS
Traditional
Blessed be the tie that binds
For the beauty of the earth
Son of God, eternal Saviour
Jesus, where'er thy people meet
Help us to help each other, Lord

Modern
Let there be love shared among us
A new commandment
As we are gathered
Bind us together
Father, make us one

CONFESSION
Eternal God, your love knows no limits and extends to all who come to you in repentance and faith. We are sorry that we have rejected your love, and not responded to your gracious words. Forgive our self-centredness and pardon our rebelliousness. Open our eyes to see the extent of your love and our hearts to receive it, so that our lives may be transformed and others

drawn into your welcoming arms for the sake of your Son, Jesus Christ our Lord, Amen.

God our loving Father have mercy on you, forgive you all your sins, bring you the joy of his salvation and restore you to his love through Christ our Lord, Amen.

INTERCESSION

Lord Jesus, we love you because you first loved us and gave your life for us. We bring you our thanksgiving and prayers, saying:
Lord Jesus, Friend of Sinners,
Help us to love you more dearly.

Lord Jesus, we ask your blessing on this church and the church throughout the world, in particular . . . We bring you our worship and service, saying:
Jesus, Saviour and Master,
Help us to love you more dearly.

Lord Jesus, we ask your blessing on those who govern us and shape our society, in particular . . . We bring you our concerns and cares, saying:
Jesus, Redeemer of the world,
Help us to love you more dearly.

Lord Jesus, we ask your blessing on the needy of our world, in particular . . . We bring you our sadness and compassion, saying:
Jesus, Light of the World,
Help us to love you more dearly.

Lord Jesus, we ask your blessing on our families and friends, and those we know who are in need, in particular . . . We bring you our homes and our community, saying:
Jesus, Healer and Deliverer,
Help us to love you more dearly.

Lord Jesus, we ask you to bless us as we follow your leading and obey your call. We bring you ourselves, just as we are, knowing that you will accept us and fill us with your unending love. Jesus, Lord and King,
Help us to see you more clearly, love your more dearly and follow you more nearly, day by day, through our Saviour Jesus Christ, Amen.

ALL-AGE ADDRESS

This idea is very simple, but takes a while to set up and prepare. Find an empty chocolate box, of the flat variety (i.e. not Roses or Quality Street). Keep the plastic inner try and refill it as follows. Using a box of chocolates such as Roses, take a few sweets and carefully unwrap them. Around each sweet wrap a piece of paper with a description of love on it from 1 Corinthians 13 – examples might be 'love is patient' or 'love is kind'. Re-wrap these in the original wrapper and replace them in the tray. At the start of the address bring out the closed box and make some comments about someone who loves you buying you chocolates. Then ask how you might know whether their love is real. Say that the evidence is in the box, and invite a few children to come and each unwrap a sweet, first reading out the wording on the inner paper before eating the chocolate. There are 15 comments made by Paul about love in this chapter, but this would lead to a very long address if you took them all separately. A suggested series of combinations might look like this:

1) Love is patient and kind. These two go well together and are inter-related. They are linked by acceptance and

understanding. Patience isn't just about not losing our temper or waiting around. Paul here is referring to a willingness to listen and accept without judgement. Kindness becomes much easier to express in that sort of relationship. We feel less inclined to be kind to those we don't really accept.

2) Love doesn't envy or boast and isn't proud. These are also connected. Boasting and pride are first cousins, but showing-off in relationships is often the result of envy. We don't like what someone else has or can do, and resent it, so we try to assert ourselves and demonstrate our 'superiority' by boasting.

3) Love is neither rude nor self-seeking, nor does it flare up in anger. Again, it's clear that these are stable-mates. Rudeness, whether in speech or behaviour, can never have the other's interests at heart, and is therefore the result of self-seeking, or putting Number One first. Sudden flare-ups of anger and irritation are invariably the result of self being dented or upset, and can never be passed off as Christian love.

4) Love doesn't store up resentment or bitterness, and rejoices in what is good, not what's wrong. It's astonishing how much easier it is to condemn someone and pull their reputation down than it is to praise and encourage them. One of the marks of Christian love is that it concentrates on the good and right and brings out the best. It certainly doesn't revel in gossip about the dark side of someone's character.

5) Love protects, trusts, hopes and perseveres – always. It doesn't give up when things get tough, and doesn't back off at the first obstacle. Rather, it keeps going, regardless of the cost.

6) Love never fails. This reiterates the previous points. End by pointing out how all of these are seen in Jesus' life, and if we claim to be his followers, they must be seen in ours too.

The Life of the Church

One of the aims of promoting all-age worship is that it's more likely to enable those who wouldn't otherwise come to church to feel at ease in a church service. For quite a few people it's proved to be the way into the Christian faith and active commitment to God's Church. They then need to have an overview of the life of the whole church and fellowship. It's important to emphasise that all-age services may be less formal or traditional, but they don't constitute an easy way to live the Christian life. Those who regularly attend them aren't exempt from the responsibilities of being a member of the whole Body of Christ.

This section therefore deals with five different aspects of the life of the Church. It's hardly exhaustive coverage, but these five topics are among the most important, and they apply to every member, not just the PCC or leadership. In an era when a word like 'commitment' is sneered at by many, the Church should be standing out in stark contrast to the prevailing apathy. There's far more to being a member of God's Kingdom than warming a pew each Sunday!

Worship

It's hardly surprising that most people's impression of the Church is based on its worship. Not only is it the 'public face' of the church, but it's also usually a barometer of the spiritual conditions there. If you ask most people what their local church is like, they'll probably tell you first, "The vicar's sermons are a bit dull", or "The singing's awful", or "The services aren't like they used to be". It may not be clear how to define a good sermon, or acceptable music, but the impression's been made. Worship, however, is far more than a good performance or a good sermon. An average sermon won't detract from worship that's alive, but the most spectacular choir and finest preacher can't breathe life into a service that's dead.

Many churchgoers (and non-churchgoers, too) tend to view worship as an 'either-or'. It's either lively or dull, traditional or modern, good or bad. It's done to the congregation by the minister and musicians, and those on the receiving end decide whether or not they like it. If not, they go and find a more acceptable variety. This is the gospel of the consumer society, which views religion, like everything else, as a sort of buffet from which folk can take their pick. Nothing could be further from the Biblical concept of worship. Nowhere do Paul or the other New Testament writers encourage their readers to look around for a church they like, or sit in judgement on those who don't do things their way. They're much more concerned to ensure that we base our worship on right beliefs about God, however we may adapt the forms in which we worship him.

More than anything else worship is in the hearts of those who come to attend a service. If they aren't worshipping God in their everyday lives they won't be able to switch it on come Sunday. Worship is the highest act we can perform or participate in as human beings. We come closest to what God made us to be when we're worshipping him. Whatever style we may adopt, whatever our cultural background and presuppositions, we're one as we come before our Creator and Redeemer. The whole church family needs to take this on board, so that Sunday services are a true reflection of the worship of our hearts day by day.

Readings
Exodus 34:1–14/Nehemiah 12:27–31, 40–43/Isaiah 44:12–23/Psalm 8/98/148/ Acts 17:22–31/Hebrews 13:7–16/ Revelation 19:1–10/Matthew 14:22–32/ Luke 4:1–13/John 4:1(or 19)–26

Hymns
Traditional
Give to our God immortal praise
Praise to the Lord, the Almighty
To God be the glory
O worship the Lord in the beauty
O worship the King

Modern
God of glory, we exalt your name
Worthy, O worthy are you, Lord
Majesty
O Lord our God (We will magnify)
Praise him on the trumpet

Confession
Almighty God, Maker of all things, you are sovereign over our world, King of Kings and Lord of Lords. You alone are worthy of our worship. We confess to you our self-will and refusal to acknowledge you as ruler of our lives. We are sorry and ashamed and ask your forgiveness. Give us a fresh vision of your glory and enable us to worship you in Spirit and truth to the glory of your Son Jesus Christ our Lord, Amen.

God our Heavenly Father in his great mercy pardon and deliver you from all your sin, open your eyes to see his majesty anew, and fill your hearts with love and worship for his Son Jesus Christ our Lord, Amen.

INTERCESSION
We kneel in awe before the Lord Almighty, acknowledging his kingship as we pray:
Sovereign Lord, open our lips,
And our mouths will proclaim your praise.

Lord of the Church, you call us to bear witness to your greatness in our worship and our witness. We pray for the Church throughout the world and for this fellowship . . . May we declare with our lives that you are our God.
Sovereign Lord, open our lips,
And our mouths will proclaim your praise.

Lord of our world, you call us to be your ambassadors, upholding the standards of your Kingdom of Light in the darkness surrounding us. We pray for the nations of the world and our own nation, and for those who govern us . . . May all people acknowledge your saving power.
Sovereign Lord, open our lips,
And our mouths will proclaim your praise.

Lord of all peace, you call us to bring your healing love to all who are in need, suffering in body, mind or spirit. We pray for those known to us . . .
May they experience the work of your Spirit in their lives.
Sovereign Lord, open our lips,
And our mouths will proclaim your praise.

Lord of our lives, you call us to worship you in everything we do, to be holy as you are holy. May others be drawn through your working in us to worship you as Lord and Saviour.
Sovereign Lord, open our lips,
And our mouths will proclaim your praise to the glory and honour of Jesus our Saviour, Amen.

ALL-AGE ADDRESS
While preparing this section I noticed in *The Times* a star-rated guide to a place of worship, a weekly column for their religious correspondent. The sermon got five stars (amazingly!) but the music only three, while the welcome merited four! This address is designed to be an antidote to such a mentality. You'll need two volunteers (one male, one female) preferably in different age-groups, but if possible in some kind of employment. A flip-chart or OHP would be an asset in itemising certain things. The idea is based on the back page of the *Sunday Times* magazine, which features "A life in the day of . . ." some well-known or noteworthy person. Ask each volunteer first about the start of their day. As they describe how a typical day starts, write down the main activities – bath or shower, brushing teeth, dressing, combing hair, breakfast, leaving for work or school. With some variations this will prove similar for both. Then ask about each volunteer's daily work, at the factory or office, at school or home. If you choose a housewife and mother emphasise how important this is as work. We work when we study and do our daily chores as much as we would in a high-powered job. Work is part of God's created order and shouldn't become a tedious grind. Finally, ask the volunteers what they

do when they come home in the evening, or at weekends. Watching TV, practising sports or a musical instrument, reading, visiting people or places might all be ways in which they relax and ease the stress in other parts of their lives. Your two volunteers should be committed Christians, because in all they've said their love for God will come through. Find out if they pray every day and read God's Word. Encourage them to say how their church life fits in with their other responsibilities.

Worship should be in every aspect of living. We can worship God by doing our work as well as we possibly can, by playing games fairly and to the full, by enjoying life in the right way, by looking for the good in every situation and person we meet, by the positive attitude which comes from the Holy Spirit living within us. Conclude by stressing that our worship in church will only be as good as our worship day by day.

Prayer

Of all the aspects of church life which might have been considered in this section none causes more vexation than prayer. This may seem odd, since prayer should be a source of peace and security rather than tension. But even the most committed of Christians will bemoan the state of their prayer life from time to time. There have been innumerable attempts to rectify this, from books which impart the 'real secret' of how to pray, to conferences and retreats which promise to revolutionise our inner life. These may be more or less successful, but there's no magic formula, no one activity or publication which will make us pray the right way ever after.

There are many approaches to prayer which could be said to 'work', but many of the problems we encounter are less to do with method than attitude. Perhaps the greatest error is to assume that prayer will do something for us, which leads to the 'shopping list' mentality. Prayer isn't like a slot machine, which requires a certain coin before you can get the product out. If we pray selfishly, looking for what benefits we might gain as a result, then as James says in his letter, we won't receive an answer because we haven't prayed with the right attitude. Prayer is a great blessing, but God wants us to communicate with him out of love, not expectation. When we come to God in prayer we enter into his way of seeing things – "May the mind of Christ my Saviour live in me from hour to hour ..." God surely answers prayer when we understand how he wants us to pray.

The other frequent misunderstanding about prayer in churches is the need for corporate as well as private prayer. Not only as individuals but also as the Body of Christ we come before God, and the latter should be emphasised strongly in our individual-oriented society. Sadly, church prayer meetings have all too often had a bad press, being perceived as a stage for the super-spiritual elite or the sounding-board for a vocal minority. On the contrary, corporate prayer in which everyone is free to take part should be a normal part of church life. That doesn't negate the value of the intercessions during an act of worship, but instead complements them, perhaps bringing before God at greater length more specific and personal needs which couldn't be addressed in public. It's significant that almost all growing churches have a lively and vigorous prayer life at their heart. Prayer life, like worship in general, is an accurate barometer of the prevailing spiritual conditions. Without that steady ongoing relationship with God there'll be no spiritual growth and no impact, either on an individual's life or on a church.

READINGS
Exodus 33:7–23/1 Kings 8:22–30/ Nehemiah 1/Psalm 17/66/143/ Philippians 4:4–9/1 Timothy 2:1–8/ James 5:13–20/Luke 11:1–13/John 14:1–13/17:1–5,20–26

HYMNS
Traditional
What a friend we have in Jesus
Prayer is the soul's sincere desire
Father, hear the prayer we offer
Lord, speak to me that I may speak
May the mind of Christ my Saviour

Modern
Father, I place into your hands
Abba Father, let me be
All Heaven waits
Make me a channel of your peace
Lord, have mercy on us

CONFESSION
Heavenly Father, we come to you in sorrow for all that we have done wrong. We repent of our sins in thought, word and deed, the result of not living in relationship with you. Forgive us, we pray, and give us courage to acknowledge our need of you, that we may turn to you in every situation and know your sustaining power, through Christ our Lord, Amen.

Almighty God, who hears the cry of all who come to him in repentance and faith, have mercy on you, pardon and deliver you from all your sin and grant you the joy of sin forgiven and the hope of eternal life for the sake of his Son Jesus Christ, Amen.

INTERCESSION
Jesus our great high priest intercedes on our behalf as we pray to God our Father, saying:
Hear us as we cry to you,
And receive our praise and prayer.

As Jesus wept over the city of Jerusalem, so he weeps over our world. Lord may we share your sorrow at the suffering in our world and your anger at the corruption . . .
Hear us as we cry to you,
And receive our praise and prayer.

As Jesus prayed for his disciples and all who follow him, so he prays on our behalf to his Father. Lord, may we be committed to the unity of the Church, and to serving the world in your name . . .
Hear us as we cry to you,
And receive our praise and prayer.

As Jesus ministered healing and deliverance to the sick and oppressed, so he still offers wholeness to all who come to him in need. Lord, may we minister healing in your name alone and bring your comfort and peace to all whose lives are troubled . . .
Hear us as we cry to you,
And receive our praise and prayer.

As Jesus called his disciples to forsake all and follow him, so he calls us to step out in faith. Lord, may we follow you without counting the cost . . .
Hear us as we cry to you,
And receive our praise and prayer for the sake of Jesus Christ our Lord, Amen.

ALL-AGE ADDRESS
For this address you'll need a household telephone (but not an answering machine), a Fax machine and a copy of a fax message, and a letter with some postage stamps. All are conveyors of messages, but unlike TV or radio, they are interactive. All three methods of communication demand a response, such as a reply to a letter, a response to a Fax message, or someone to pick up and answer the telephone. Without the two-way communication they'd be useless.

1) Start with the telephone and ask the congregation how they would use it. Speaking with a friend or relative, giving someone an urgent message, or finding something out are the replies you're likely to get. But it's no use unless someone answers. When we come to God in prayer, it may be in a crisis, it may be to ask for help or guidance, or it may simply be to tell him about our lives. God doesn't have an answering machine. He's always there to hear us when we cry out to him.

2) The Fax machine is the next illustration. Point out how essential it is to have a similar machine at the other end. Ask what a Fax might be used for, and you'll probably get a reply about business messages and documents. The great advantage of a Fax is that it's much quicker than a letter. When we pray to God, we don't have to wait to see if the message gets there in due course – God knows our prayers before we even pray them. Our messages get through straight away to God.

3) Finally display the letter and ask what you'd use the post for. There may be a variety of answers, but one of the likeliest is communicating with friends and family. God isn't only interested in our problems and crises, nor with just the big events of life. He wants to be in every part of our living, even the ordinary everyday activities like driving, catching the train, washing up or gardening. As a conclusion, emphasise that we need to receive as well as give communication. God will speak to us if we listen for his voice within us. Prayer is a two-way process of communication; just as we'd listen as well as talk in a telephone conversation, so we must listen to what God is saying to us.

Eucharist

Jesus died to bring reconciliation and unity between mankind and God and between fellow human beings. There are few more potent pictures of this than worshippers kneeling together at the altar-rail to receive the bread and wine, regardless of any differences in background, education, status, race or temperament. In Christ we're all one. The Church has never found it very easy to act this out, however. 1 Corinthians 11 makes it clear that Paul was aware of all kinds of problems in that church, while the Reformation resulted in more ink being spilled on the subject of the Eucharist (Mass, Holy Communion or Lord's Supper, whichever you prefer) than on anything else in the Church's history. The term Eucharist will be used here, partly because it's neutral in terms of church tradition, but mainly because it means in Greek 'thanksgiving'. This isn't the place to re-enter the controversy about what might happen to the bread and wine during the service. Instead we can concentrate on the different elements of the service, looking at them as essential components of the whole.

There's been a major shift in perceptions about the place of the Eucharist in parish life. The Parish Communion movement has resulted in many Church of England parishes regarding the Eucharist as the main act of worship each week. Family Communion has become an acceptable, and often desirable occasion for families to come before God's table together, to such an extent that the idea of allowing children to take bread and wine before Confirmation is gaining wide currency in the Church of England. All this, however, puts a premium on the meaning of the Eucharist being explained simply and clearly. Worshippers need to understand not the detailed theology so much as the personal application of it. God's Table is open to all; no-one should feel debarred or rejected. For most it's the supreme experience of their relationship with Christ, when they not only remember his death for them, but also receive his grace and risen power into their lives. The Eucharist should never be marginalised or kept out of the mainstream of the Church's life. Rather it should be the unifying factor and focal point of the life of the whole fellowship.

READINGS
Genesis 14:17–20/Exodus 12:14–28/
Isaiah 25:6–9/Psalm 36/41/116/
1 Corinthians 11:17–26 (or 34)/Acts
2:42–47/Hebrews 9:15–24/Matthew
26:17–30/John 6:25–35/15:1–8

HYMNS
Traditional
Here, O my Lord, I see thee face to
 face
Jesus, stand among us
We come as guests invited
We hail thy presence glorious
And now, O Father, mindful of the
 love

Modern
Broken for me
We break this bread*
I am the Bread of Life
There is a Redeemer
Take, eat, this is my body

* The Anglican Rite 'A' service has
been attractively set by Chris Rolinson –
much of the music is in Songs Of
Fellowship or Mission Praise.

CONFESSION
**Lord Jesus, you gave your life for us
that we might be set free, yet we have**

spurned your love, and remain in the chains of sin. Forgive our stubbornness and pride and make us receptive to your saving grace. Release us from our bondage to sin and set us free to worship and serve you in love and joy through the death and resurrection of our Lord Jesus Christ, Amen.

God our Father, who in His Son Jesus Christ has won for us forgiveness and new life, have mercy on you, pardon you for all your sins, restore you to the fellowship of his table and bring you at last to his heavenly banquet for the sake of his Son Jesus Christ, our Saviour, Amen.

INTERCESSION

We come to the table prepared for us by our heavenly King, bringing our prayers and thanksgiving.
Lord Jesus, you are the Way, the Truth and the Life,
Lead us in the way everlasting.

We thank you for guiding your flock throughout its history. We ask you to bless your people here . . . and throughout the world . . . Teach us to listen to your voice and follow the path you show us.
Lord Jesus, you are the Good Shepherd,
Keep us in the way everlasting.

We thank you that you are the sovereign Lord of all. We ask you to lead those who rule this world in the ways of righteousness and peace . . . Teach them to obey your commands and uphold your laws.
Lord Jesus, you are the Light of the World,
Shine on us in the way everlasting.

We thank you for your care and compassion for all who suffer in body or mind. We ask you to comfort and heal any who are known to us . . . Teach them to trust you in their sorrows and hold on to you in adversity.
Lord Jesus, you are the Bread of Life,
Sustain us in the way everlasting.

We thank you for your Holy Spirit who strengthens and enables us to do your will. We ask you to keep us firm in our faith and witness . . . Teach us to find in you our all in all and look to you for help.
Lord Jesus, you are the Vine,
Refresh us in the way everlasting.

We thank you for all who have walked the Pilgrim path before us . . . We ask you to help us respond to the challenge of their lives . . . Teach us to forget what is behind and reach out for what lies ahead. Lord Jesus, you are the Resurrection and the Life,
Keep us in the way everlasting until our journey's end, when we see you face to face, our Saviour, Guide and Friend, Jesus Christ, Amen.

ALL-AGE ADDRESS

Unlike most all-age addresses, this one needs no visual aids, as the symbols of Holy Communion speak for themselves. It also comes in several short sections, fitted in before each main part of the Eucharist. In order to focus attention on the service rather than the address, these sections should be brief. The thread that holds everything together is friendship – our friendship with God the Father through Jesus Christ and our friendship with one another.

1) Friends are usually pretty obvious to others because they enjoy each other's company. As God's friends we come to enjoy being with him and with each other. As we recall God's love for us, so we express our love for him in worship and praise as we sing hymns.

2) Friends sometimes fall out or argue and have to say sorry. We have to confess our sins to God whenever we come before him, and receive his forgiveness. A broken relationship has to be put right before it can continue and grow. In repenting of what we've done wrong, we allow God to restore our friendship with him and heal the consequences of our failures.

3) Friends listen to each other. We listen to God's voice particularly through the reading of Scripture and its explanation in the sermon or address.

4) Friends talk to one another and share their lives. When we come to God in prayer that's exactly what we do, telling God what's on our hearts and listening to what is on his heart. Prayer is a dialogue.

5) Because we're God's friends he wants us to get along with one another as he does with us, forgiving and accepting. In the Peace we acknowledge that we come before God as one people, united in worship and service, and putting aside our differences.

6) Friends share a meal together. God wants us to share in his feast, a foretaste of the Heavenly banquet to which we're all invited. When we come to his table we catch a glimpse of what Heaven will be like, with everyone kneeling before God in adoration, oblivious of differences.

7) Friends want to see each other again and look forward to the next meeting. Each of these points can be made before the relevant part of the service and elaborated a little. Clearly there's no need for a sermon as well, because the explanation serves that purpose. This is an idea worth repeating every so often, to dispel any fears or misunderstandings about the Eucharist and make it accessible to everyone.

Evangelism

At the time of writing we're well into the Decade of Evangelism. The whole Church throughout the world has been encouraged by its leaders to spread the good news of Jesus Christ wherever it has the opportunity. Perhaps the oddest thing is that it all sounds like a twentieth century invention! For many years evangelism was widely regarded as 'bad form', an activity to be engaged in only by those with more zeal than brain. It became the preserve of con-men and lunatics, typified by Elmer Gantry. More recently, however, the Church has discovered that if there's no evangelism there's a rapidly declining church, and soon no church at all. William Temple once pointed out that the Church 'is a club which exists exclusively for the benefit of its non-members'. The Early Church certainly took Christ's 'great commission' to heart. By the end of the first century the gospel had spread from its roots in a provincial backwater of the Roman Empire as far as North Africa, Italy, and eastwards too. Two hundred years later much of Europe and North Africa had flourishing churches, the result of Christians travelling along the trade routes, talking about their faith as they went. For an organisation that started with twelve frightened and uneducated men, it did astonishingly well, soon becoming the largest and most powerful religious influence in the world.

As the Church has forgotten its origins so it's declined, at least in the 'advanced' western world. The Church has grown most in Third World countries, and in places where Christianity has no long-term history or influence, such as Uganda, the Philippines and South Korea. The Church in Zaire has experienced significant growth in recent years because of the enthusiastic evangelism of Christian re-fugees from neighbouring Uganda. But evangelism isn't just for a few experts and neither is it the result of specially learned techniques. It doesn't involve manipulation or deceit, nor is it interested in making money. It happens quite naturally as the Holy Spirit is released in God's people, as he was in the disciples on the day of Pentecost. Every church and every believer is charged with fulfilling the great commission, to bring the Gospel to everyone. It isn't a task that finishes at the end of the decade!

READINGS
2 Kings 6:24–25,7:3–11/Ecclesiastes 7:8–14/Isaiah 52:7–10/Psalm 40:1–10/ 71:14–24/96/Acts 14:1–7/2 Corinthians 4:1–6/1 John 1/Matthew 10:1–10/Mark 1:14–28/Luke 4:14–21

HYMNS
Traditional
O for a thousand tongues to sing
We have a gospel to proclaim
Tell out, my soul
Ye servants of God
Send forth the gospel

Modern
One shall tell another
Make way, make way
We'll walk the land
From the sun's rising
How lovely on the mountains

CONFESSION
Lord Jesus, you came to bring good news to the poor, to proclaim the Kingdom of God. Our tongues have been still and our lips silent when we might have extolled your Name. Father, forgive our reluctance, **Fill our lips with your praise.**

Our actions have been thoughtless
and our lives self-centred. Father,
forgive our disobedience,
Fill our hearts with your love.

Our thoughts have been far from you
and our minds on this world only.
Father, forgive our arrogance,
Fill our minds with your truth.

Our witness has been half-hearted
and our boldness diminished.
Father, forgive our lack of
commitment,
**Fill our lives with your love and joy,
that in worship we may honour you,
in service we may proclaim you and in
witness we may declare the glory of
him who died for our freedom, Jesus
Christ our Lord, Amen.**

INTERCESSION

Mighty God, you have commanded
your Church to spread your name to
every people and culture, tradition
and background. The fields are white
to harvest but the workers are few. We
pray for those who are labouring for
the Gospel, in whatever situation you
have called them, among rich or poor,
young or old, white or black. Help
them to declare your truth boldly yet
sensitively, powerfully yet gently, that
the good news of your salvation and
love may reach ears that have never
heard it. We pray too for more of your
people to respond to the need to
proclaim your praise to all mankind.
May we with them see a mighty
harvest brought into your kingdom for
the sake of Jesus Christ our Saviour,
Amen.

Lord Jesus, you commissioned your
disciples to preach the Gospel
throughout the world, to every race,
colour, culture and tradition. Your
saving love extends to all people,
regardless of human divisions and
barriers. As we seek to obey your
command to make disciples, help us to
recognise the attitudes in us which
cause us to make wrong distinctions,
so that all have an equal opportunity
to respond to your gracious invitation
to eternal life in Jesus Christ our Lord,
Amen.

Father of all, we pray for your Church
throughout the world as it takes the
good news of Jesus to places in
desperate need. Especially we pray for
. . . We pray too for those who
minister to the homeless, the poverty-
stricken, the unemployed and the
lonely, that through them the message
of hope and eternal life may shine in
the darkness and despair . . . Join us
together in the task of evangelism,
that we and all your people may
rejoice to see your Kingdom extended
and your name glorified, Amen.

ALL-AGE ADDRESS

Even in the 'liveliest' of churches
there'll be many who feel uneasy
when they hear the word 'evangelism'. For some it implies unscrupulous
frauds, for others a below-the-belt
manipulation of feelings. On the other
side of the coin there are churches
who give the impression that evangelism is a kind of spiritual scalp-hunt! In
one sense it isn't a church 'activity' at
all. Like prayer, it's a natural outflow
from living the Christian life, an integral part of our faith. All Christians are
called to it in one form or another, and
while there are those with a specific
evangelistic ministry, they rely for the
most part on the day-by-day witness
of believers at work and at home, in
society and in the local community.

This address is based on the true meaning of evangelism, in Greek 'good news'. The idea comes from the popular TV quiz 'Have I Got News for You', though without the 'near-the-knuckle' comments and heavy satire which characterise it. It needs some preliminary preparation and a flip-chart or OHP.

1) Two or three volunteers should be sat in front of the congregation as the 'contestants'. The first game is to identify an event from a headline, which can be displayed on the flip-chart or OHP. Examples might be 'Lame man walks on air after coming to earth with a bump' (the paralysed man lowered through the roof in front of Jesus); 'vintage performance' (the water changed into wine); 'bread mountain' (the feeding of the five thousand); 'government attacked over exploitation' (referring to a number of Jesus' disputes with the authorities). Alternatively, in the lead-up to Easter you could use a sequence of headlines – 'Jesus arrested in surprise move'; 'followers in the dark' (Jesus' trial was held at night); 'nationalist freed as crowd riots' (Barabbas' release); 'earthquake rocks city as traitor put to death'; 'soldiers charged with sleeping as body goes missing'. Whether you use these or invent your own, ensure that you finish with the passion and resurrection, explaining that Jesus' death wasn't in itself good news, but that we can all be forgiven as a result and set free from our sins and their consequences.

2) The second game is to supply a caption to a picture. This needs some prior artwork, however simple. Examples could include Jesus changing the water into wine, the calming of the storm on Galilee, the calling of the disciples, Jesus' temptations or some other event in his life. Having previously seen the pictures on an OHP slide or flip-chart, make sure you've thought of some captions too. Again, finish with the Cross, so that the captions indicate somehow what God is saying to us through the death of his Son.

3) Finally, 'what happened next?' Narrate an account of a miracle or parable of Jesus in a twentieth century idiom, but stop before the end and ask the 'contestants' what happened next. As before, finish with Jesus on the Cross, but wait for someone to point out the resurrection as the next event. Show how 'what happened next' was always part of God's plan for mankind. Jesus' death is good news for all of us, because it means forgiveness, freedom and new life. Why not share it?

Service

The idea of service will appeal to the British sense of 'doing one's duty'. It could easily be presented as a dreary chore – a 'necessary evil' in life. No-one could reasonably deny that good works aren't the sole preserve of Christians. Plenty of good is done by those who make no claims to adhering to the Christian faith. Sometimes the Church is embarrassed by the social conscience seen in the rest of the world, because it hasn't reacted as it should in particular circumstances. However, Christian service is far more than helping the elderly or caring for the sick. In serving God we're expressing in practical terms our love of God. Just as he is compassionate and merciful, so are we if his love fills our lives. There are many ways to do this in the community. Some will feel drawn to caring for the elderly or the handicapped. Some will recognise that their ministry lies with those who are ill or dying. Others will feel God moving them to work among the homeless or poverty-stricken, the unemployed or exploited. Yet others will be able to serve God in spheres of significant influence, either in government or in commerce and industry. Healing and counselling, administering or organising, the list is endless, because God wants us to serve him and witness for him in every stratum of society, in every aspect of life. There are specific forms of service related to the local church, but those certainly shouldn't exclude the service of our daily lives, wherever we're called to lead them. Having said that, the church corporately should be serving God in its local community. This isn't a paternalistic approach but one rooted in Scripture. If someone in the fellowship or local community is bereaved, who gets alongside them? If an elderly person needs transport to the surgery, who's first to volunteer? If a young Mum has just returned from hospital, who'll offer to prepare an evening meal? It should be a natural outcome of the Christian life being lived, that members of the local church will be in the forefront in such situations.

Another part of service is the willingness to speak out for those who have no voice, to act for those who have no power. The Church has a strong voice even today in challenging evil, greed and selfishness. Just as Jesus lived for other people so do we in obedience to his command. As he said, denying self is the only way to find it.

READINGS
Deuteronomy 15:1–11/Proverbs 31:10–20/Isaiah 42:1–9/Psalm 72/82/119:105–112/Acts 6:1–7/2 Corinthians 9:6–15/Colossians 3:18–25/Matthew 6:19–24/25:31–46/Mark 10:35–45/John 13:1–17

HYMNS
Traditional
Teach me, my God and King
All to Jesus I surrender
O Thou, who camest from above
Strengthen for service, Lord, the hands
O Jesus, I have promised

Modern
I want to walk with Jesus Christ
Send me out from here, Lord
I want to serve the purpose of God
When I needed a neighbour
Seek ye first the kingdom of God.

CONFESSION
Lord Jesus, you came to be the servant of all, and to give your life for others. Forgive our selfishness and blindness to the needs of others and deliver us from the consequences of our thoughtlessness. We are truly sorry

and ask you to reorder our lives so that you take first place. Give us your servant heart that we may rejoice to do your will for the sake of Jesus Christ, the servant of all, Amen.

God our Father, who redeemed us regardless of the cost, have mercy on you, pardon and deliver you from all self-will and self-centredness, fill you with his love and strength and bring you to his eternal home, through Jesus Christ our Lord, Amen.

INTERCESSION
We bow before the Sovereign Lord, whose service is perfect freedom, saying:
Servant King as we live for you,
May we serve you gladly.

Lord Jesus, we are your people, called to do your will. May we and all your Church recognise your voice as we bear witness to your unending love. Especially we pray for . . .
Servant King as we live for you,
May we serve you willingly.

Lord Jesus, we are your ambassadors, members of your Kingdom in a godless world. May we uphold your commandments and delight in your laws as we seek to influence our community and society. Especially we pray for . . .
Servant King as we live for you,
May we serve you wholeheartedly.

Lord Jesus, we are your hands and voice, bringing healing and hope to the suffering and downtrodden. May we reach out to them and enable them to recognise your touch upon their lives. Especially we pray for . . .
Servant King as we live for you,
May we serve you sensitively.

Lord Jesus, we are your servants, equipped by your Holy Spirit for the ministry you have entrusted to us. May we fulfil your calling with commitment and joy for as long as we live.
Servant King as we live for you,
May we serve you willingly and obediently for the sake of your Son, Jesus Christ our Lord, Amen.

ALL-AGE ADDRESS
This idea picks up on one aspect of the 'service' theme, namely serving food, and uses it to draw out what it means to serve God. Some preparation is necessary, since it relies on some volunteers acting out a restaurant scene. A written out script isn't strictly needed, but might be useful if the participants are unsure of how to ad-lib. Since the dialogue is very basic, scripts should be ultra-simple if used.

1) Ask the actors to enact a scene in which two diners give their order but are served by the waiter/waitress with something different. The diners will naturally be indignant that their order was ignored. Good restaurant service depends on the orders being properly fulfilled. Customers won't return if this doesn't happen! Point out that if we're to be good servants of Jesus we must obey our Father's orders, just as Jesus did. It's no good doing something else, however useful or nice it may seem.

2) Next ask the volunteers to build up a dialogue in which the food is ordered, and brought to the table, but served in a very rough way (e.g. thumb in soup etc). Again the diners will be annoyed and complain about the service. The point is clear enough.

Poor service is as bad as no service at all. God isn't pleased if we serve him with grumpy faces and hearts, or only half do what he wants us to. If we listen to our orders properly and love God, we'll want to serve him with all our hearts, to the best of our ability and in his strength, so that his work is done well and his name glorified as a result.

3) The third scene is of two diners who place their orders only for the waiter/waitress to refuse until more money is handed over. You'll hardly need to explain why the diners are irritated on this occasion! Show how God wants us to serve him because we love him, not for how much more we can get out of him. Jesus was the servant of all and went to the Cross for our sakes, willingly and lovingly. He put his own interests to the bottom of the pile, and those who follow his way must do likewise.

4) As a coda, ask the actors finally to do the job properly, and enact a happy scene in which table service is excellent and the diners delighted. Point out that willing service can change relationships and bring joy and happiness to both servant and served. God doesn't force us to serve him. Rather, he wants us to do so out of love for him and our fellow human beings.

Resources

There are so many different resources now available, that it seems invidious to single any out. However, the following suggestions may prove useful:

MUSIC:
  Mission Praise (combined volume)
  Hymns Ancient & Modern New
    Standard
  Hymns for Today's Church
  Songs and Hymns of Fellowship
    (combined volumes 1–4)
  Hymns Old & New

Most of the suggested hymns and songs come from one of these volumes. Much new material is being produced, some of which is of high quality. The Christian Music Association licensing system does not cover every item in these books, so please ensure that you know what is covered, so that you stay within the law. There are such a large number of musical resources that the only recommendation is to beware of the quality!

PRAYERS:
  Patterns for Worship
  Prayers for the People –
    ed. M. Perry
  Springboard for Worship –
    Susan Sayers

Again, there are innumerable volumes of prayers and liturgical material. Each church will have its own style and taste in such matters, but as well as prayers, there are other items such as Affirmations of Faith, Introductory Sentences and spoken words of praise, which can all be used to add variety and richness.